T0114816

GRADE **1**

ENGAGE THE BRAIN GAMES

MARCIA L. TATE

CORWIN PRESS
Classroom

For information:

Corwin Press
A SAGE Company
2455 Teller Road
Thousand Oaks, California 91320
CorwinPress.com

SAGE, Ltd.
1 Oliver's Yard
55 City Road
London EC1Y 1SP
United Kingdom

SAGE India Pvt. Ltd.
B 1/I 1 Mohan Cooperative
Industrial Area
Mathura Road, New Delhi
India 110 044

SAGE Asia-Pacific Pvt. Ltd.
33 Pekin Street #02-01
Far East Square
Singapore 048763

ISBN: 978-1-4129-5932-2

This book is printed on acid-free paper.

08 09 10 11 12 10 9 8 7 6 5 4 3 2 1

Executive Editor: Kathleen Hex
Managing Developmental Editor: Christine Hood
Editorial Assistant: Anne O'Dell
Developmental Writer: Jeanine Manfro
Developmental Editor: Karen Sandoval
Proofreader: Mary Barbosa
Art Director: Anthony D. Paular
Design Project Manager: Jeffrey Stith
Cover Designers: Lisa Miller and Monique Hahn
Illustrator: Patty Briles
Cover Illustrator: Jenny Campbell
Design Consultant: The Development Source

GRADE **1**

TABLE OF CONTENTS

Connections to Standards

This chart shows the national academic standards covered in each chapter.

LANGUAGE ARTS	Standards are covered on pages
Read a wide range of print and nonprint texts to build an understanding of texts, of self, and of the cultures of the United States and the world; to acquire new information; to respond to the needs and demands of society and the workplace; and for personal fulfillment (includes fiction and nonfiction, classic, and contemporary works).	20, 22
Read a wide range of literature from many periods in many genres to build an understanding of the many dimensions (e.g., philosophical, ethical, aesthetic) of human experience.	20
Apply a wide range of strategies to comprehend, interpret, evaluate, and appreciate texts. Draw on prior experience, interactions with other readers and writers, knowledge of word meaning and of other texts, word identification strategies, and understanding of textual features (e.g., sound-letter correspondence, sentence structure, context, graphics).	9, 13, 15
Adjust the use of spoken, written, and visual language (e.g., conventions, style, vocabulary) to communicate effectively with a variety of audiences and for different purposes.	20, 22
Apply knowledge of language structure, language conventions (e.g., spelling and punctuation), media techniques, figurative language, and genre to create, critique, and discuss print and nonprint texts.	9, 13, 15, 25

MATHEMATICS	Standards are covered on pages
Number and Operations—Understand numbers, ways of representing numbers, relationships among numbers, and number systems.	27, 31, 35
Number and Operations—Understand meanings of operations and how they relate to one another.	31, 35
Number and Operations—Compute fluently and make reasonable estimates.	31, 35
Geometry—Analyze characteristics and properties of two- and three-dimensional geometric shapes and develop mathematical arguments about geometric relationships.	43
Geometry—Apply transformations and use symmetry to analyze mathematical situations.	43
Geometry—Use visualization, spatial reasoning, and geometric modeling to solve problems.	43

978-1-4129-5932-2

Measurement—Understand measurable attributes of objects and the units, systems, and processes of measurement.	38
Measurement—Apply appropriate techniques, tools, and formulas to determine measurements.	38
Data Analysis and Probability—Select and use appropriate statistical methods to analyze data.	38

SCIENCE	Standards are covered on pages
Physical Science—Understand properties of objects and materials.	48
Life Science—Understand characteristics of organisms.	50
Life Science—Understand organisms and environments.	55
Earth and Space Science—Understand changes in the earth and sky.	58

SOCIAL STUDIES	Standards are covered on pages
Understand culture and culture diversity.	66, 72
Understand the ways human beings view themselves in and over time.	72
Understand interactions among people, places, and environments.	62, 66
Understand individual development and identity.	70
Understand interactions among individuals, groups, and institutions.	62, 66
Understand how people organize for the production, distribution, and consumption of goods and services.	76
Understand the ideals, principles, and practices of citizenship in a democratic republic.	62, 70

Introduction

An ancient Chinese proverb claims: "Tell me, I forget. Show me, I remember. Involve me, I understand." This timeless saying insinuates what all educators should know: Unless students are involved and actively engaged in learning, true learning rarely occurs.

The latest brain research reveals that both the right and left hemispheres of the brain should be engaged in the learning process. This is important because the hemispheres talk to one another over the corpus callosum, the structure that connects them.

Using learning games is a valid and important teaching strategy. The mechanisms involved when students are playing a game are just as cognitive as when students are doing math seatwork (Bjorkland & Brown, 1998). Furthermore, play speeds up the brain's maturation process because it involves the built-in processes of challenge, novelty, feedback, coherence, and time (Jensen, 2001).

How to Use This Book

The activities in this book cover the content areas and are designed using strategies that actively engage the brain. They are presented in the way the brain learns best to make sure students get the most out of each lesson: focus activity, modeling, guided practice, check for understanding, independent practice, and closing. Go through each step to ensure that students will be fully engaged in the concept being taught and understand its purpose and meaning.

Each step-by-step activity provides a game that students can use to reinforce learning. Students will enjoy playing variations of classic games such as Go Fish, 20 Questions, Telephone, Follow the Leader, Bingo, relay races, memory matching, and more!

Games can be lively, fun, and spirited. The little bit of extra effort it takes to implement games into your curriculum will reap loads in student involvement. Because games can create lots of excitement and healthy rivalry, make sure to set firm ground rules before playing any classroom game.

These brain-compatible activities are sure to engage and motivate every student's brain in your classroom! Watch students progress from passive to active learners as they process competitive, exciting games into learning that is not only fun, but remembered for a lifetime.

Put It Into Practice

Lecture and repetitive worksheets have long been the traditional method of delivering knowledge and reinforcing learning. While some higher-achieving students may engage in this type of learning, educators now know that actively engaging students' brains is not a luxury, but a necessity if students are truly to acquire and retain content, not only for tests but for life.

The 1990s were dubbed the Decade of the Brain because millions of dollars were spent on brain research. Educators today should know more about how students learn than ever before. Learning styles theories that call for student engagement have been proposed for decades, as evidenced by research such as Howard Gardner's theory of multiple intelligences (1983), Bernice McCarthy's 4MAT Model (1990), and VAKT (visual, auditory, kinesthetic, tactile) learning styles theories.

I have identified 20 strategies that, according to brain research and learning styles theories, appear to correlate with the way the brain learns best. I have observed hundreds of teachers—regular education, special education, and gifted. Regardless of the classification or grade level of the students, exemplary teachers consistently use these 20 strategies to deliver memorable classroom instruction and help their students understand and retain vast amounts of content.

These 20 brain-based instructional strategies include the following:

1. Brainstorming and Discussion

2. Drawing and Artwork

3. Field Trips

4. Games

5. Graphic Organizers, Semantic Maps, and Word Webs

6. Humor

7. Manipulatives, Experiments, Labs, and Models

8. Metaphors, Analogies, and Similes

9. Mnemonic Devices

10. Movement

11. Music, Rhythm, Rhyme, and Rap

12. Project-based and Problem-based Instruction

13. Reciprocal Teaching and Cooperative Learning

978-1-4129-5932-2

14. Role Play, Drama, Pantomime, Charades

15. Storytelling

16. Technology

17. Visualization and Guided Imagery

18. Visual Aids

19. Work Study and Apprenticeships

20. Writing and Journals

This book features Instructional Strategy 4: Games. Through play, people fulfill the body's need to express emotions, to bond with others socially, and to explore new learning with challenge, feedback, and success (Beyers, 1998). When students are given the opportunity to redesign a game with which they are already familiar, such as Go Fish, Follow the Leader, or Bingo, brain connections are made for a better understanding of the alternate content (Jensen, 1995).

Games involve active learning. They motivate students by making learning fun and engaging. In today's fast-paced world, students are frequently asked to change gears quickly, jumping from one activity to another, sometimes with little time in between to process what they have learned. Using games as a teaching strategy makes sense. Students thrive on the novelty of game playing and the quick action often associated with games. Playing learning games allows students to actively rehearse information they are expected to know in a non-threatening atmosphere. Furthermore, when students are involved in the design and construction of a learning game, the game's effectiveness is enhanced (Wolfe, 2001).

Types of effective learning games include board games, card games, memory games, trivia games, games that encourage physicality, games that involve using the senses, games that involve creative imagination, and many more.

These memorable strategies help students make sense of learning by focusing on the ways the brain learns best. Fully supported by the latest brain research, the games presented in this resource provide the tools you need to boost motivation, energy, and most important, the academic achievement of your students.

CHAPTER 1

Language Arts

Wacky Words Beanbag Toss

Objectives

Students will identify rhyming words.
Students will read simple, one-syllable words and sight words.

Students love tongue twisters and silly rhymes. Put aside the traditional pencil-and-paper worksheets, and invite students to practice identifying rhyming words with this engaging game. They'll enjoy using their brains *and* their bodies!

Materials

• Wacky Words Scorecard reproducible
• butcher paper
• index cards
• tape
• beanbags

1. Ahead of time, prepare a game board for each group of four students. Use a marker to draw a grid on a sheet of butcher paper. For students who are skilled at tossing objects with good aim, make the squares on the grid smaller. For students who are not as skilled, make the squares a bit larger. Each sheet of butcher paper should have at least 20 squares.

2. Say sentences that include rhyming words from the word families you want to focus on. For example: *The fat cat sat on the mat.* Ask students what they notice about the sentence. *(Many of the words end with the same sound.)* Invite volunteers to name other rhyming words.

3. Tell students they will be playing a game that involves rhyming words and that you need their help in creating it. Say a word from one of your chosen word families. For example, if the word family is *-ig*, you might say *big*. Ask volunteers to name rhyming words. Record each word on a separate index card.

4. Continue saying and recording rhyming words from each chosen word family. Then divide the class into groups of four. Group students together based on their skill level in aiming and throwing.

5. Give each group a butcher paper grid and 20 word cards. Groups should have at least two rhyming words from each word family.

6. Help groups tape the index cards to their grid, one word per square, in any order. Give each group a copy of the **Wacky Words Scorecard reproducible (page 12)**. Then explain the rules of the game.

   a. Teams place the butcher paper three to six feet in front of the starting line. Players line up behind the starting line.

   b. The first player tosses a beanbag onto the grid and reads the word aloud. Then he or she finds a rhyming word on the grid and tries to toss a second beanbag on it.

   c. If the second beanbag lands on a rhyming word, the player scores one point. He or she then gets to take a second turn. After the second turn, the next player in line takes a turn and the first player goes to the end of the line.

   d. If a beanbag lands on a line, the toss does not count. The player gets two more chances to toss the beanbag into a square without touching a line.

   e. The first player to score ten points wins the game. Players record their points with tally marks on the scorecard.

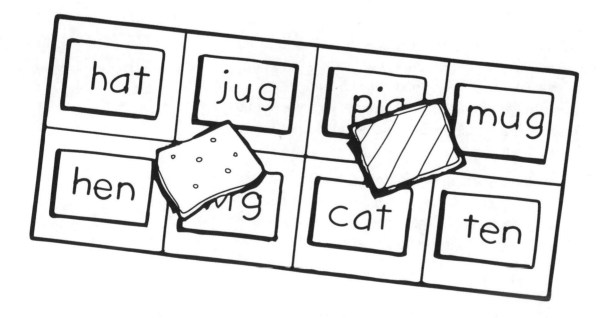

978-1-4129-5932-2

7. Model how to toss a beanbag on a grid. Say the word and ask students which word you should try to hit next. Make sure students understand the rules of the game before they play independently.

8. Circulate among the groups during game time. Answer any questions that come up and provide encouragement.

9. As a follow-up, invite students to join you in a circle. Have them name rhyming words. The last student to name a word for each word family returns to his or her seat until all students are seated again.

Extended Learning

- Have students use the word cards to play a memory match game with rhyming words.

- Encourage students to make rhyming dictionaries. Have them create lists of rhyming words for word families from the game. Invite students to illustrate their words.

Name _____ Date _____

Wacky Words Scorecard

Directions: Write the names of the players. Use tally marks for each player's points.

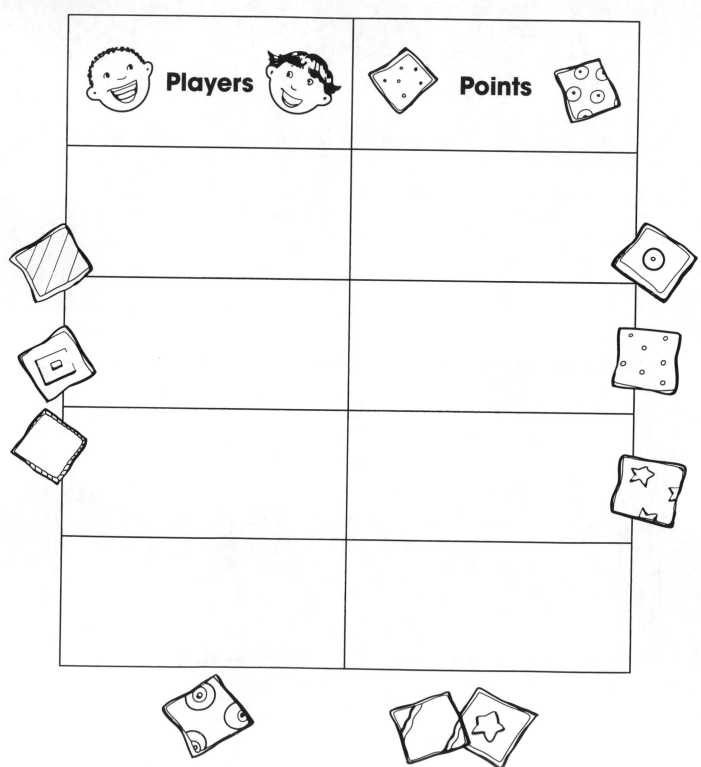

"Make the Change" Relay Race

Objectives
Students will change one letter in a word to make a new word.
Students will read simple, one-syllable words and sight words.

Put a new spin on the tried-and-true relay race. Students work in teams as they use their phonetic skills to create new words, one letter at a time.

1. Get students warmed up for this activity with a simple demonstration. Say a one-syllable word such as *cat*. Write the word on the board. Tell students: *If I change **c** to **r**, I get **rat**.* Cross out the *c* and write the word *rat* underneath *cat*. Then demonstrate another change by replacing the *t* in *rat* with *n* to spell *ran*. Now ask students if they can change the letter *a* to make a new word. Record their suggestions.

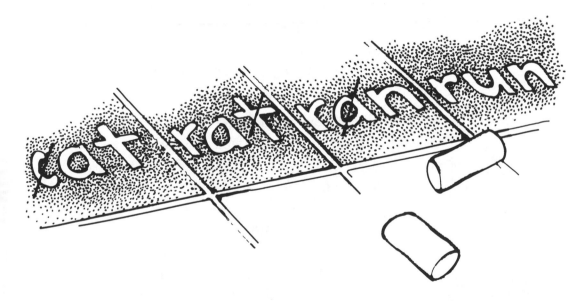

2. Explain to students that they will compete in a relay race to change one letter of a word at a time to create a new word. Divide the class into four to six teams, and take the teams outside.

3. Use chalk to draw a starting line on the ground (the blacktop or any other paved surface). Have each team line up single file behind the line.

4. Walk about ten yards above the starting line and draw another line on the ground. This is the fault line. During the relay race, runners must cross the fault line before working with the words.

5. Write a one-syllable word for each team about three feet above the fault line. The words should be spaced at least three feet apart.

6. Explain and model the rules of the game.

   a. The first player in line runs from the starting line and crosses the fault line. The player then reads the word to his or her team, crosses out one letter, and chooses another letter to make a new word. The player writes the new word below the first one and then runs to the end of the team line.

   b. The next player in line then takes a turn.

   c. The race continues until everyone on the team has had two turns changing a word.

   d. A word cannot be repeated at any time during the race.

   e. If players cannot figure out how to change a word, they can request help from a team member. To request help, players call out the name of a teammate, and that player runs from the starting line to the fault line to offer help.

   f. The first team to complete the race with no repeated words wins the game.

7. Point to a word, and ask students to suggest letters they could use to replace the first letter. Repeat with other words and suggestions for changing the middle or last letter. Make sure everyone understands the rules of the game. Then start the race. Stand near the fault line, and assist students as needed.

8. Close the activity by having students stand in a circle. Say a word such as *sun*. Ask the student standing on your left to change one letter to make a new word (e.g., change *s* to *f* to make *fun*). Continue around the circle until everyone has a turn.

Extended Learning

- Say a one-syllable word, and have students write it on paper. Set a timer for one minute. Challenge students to create as many new words they can in one minute by changing one letter at a time.

- Instead of just changing a letter in a word, encourage students to create new words by adding or deleting letters. For example, by adding letters, *sand* becomes *stand* and *stand* becomes *strand*. By deleting letters, *train* becomes *rain* and *rain* becomes *ran*.

978-1-4129-5932-2

"An Apple a Day" Memory Match

Objectives
Students will combine two smaller words to make one compound word.
Students will read and write compound words.

Materials
- An Apple a Day reproducible
- Apple Leaf Patterns reproducible
- scissors
- file folders
- glue
- dry-erase markers

When students have the opportunity to help create a learning game, the effectiveness of that game is enhanced. After helping to construct a board game, students learn about compound words as they play a matching game with partners.

1. Ahead of time, make a copy of the **An Apple a Day reproducible (page 18)** for each student. Cut out the apple shapes. Make a copy of the **Apple Leaf Patterns reproducible (page 19)** for every two students. Cut out the leaf shapes.

2. Tell students: *Listen to these words. Tell me how these words are alike:* **baseball, flashlight, toothbrush**. (They are compound words. They are made up of two smaller words.) Write the words on the board. Invite volunteers to help you brainstorm other compound words to add to the list. (See the word box on page 17 for suggestions.)

3. Divide the class into student pairs. Give each pair a file folder, 12 apple cutouts, and 24 leaf cutouts. Tell students to glue six apple cutouts on each half of the file folder. Laminate the file folders so students can write on them with dry-erase markers.

4. Choose a compound word from the class list. Model how to write each part of the word on a leaf cutout. Then have pairs choose 12 words from the list and write them on their leaf cutouts.

5. Explain and model the rules of the game.
   a. One player shuffles the leaf cutouts and places them facedown in rows.
   b. Each player chooses one-half of the file folder as his or her game board.
   c. The first player chooses two leaf cutouts, turns them faceup, and reads the words aloud.
   d. If the two words form a compound word, the player places the leaves on an apple on his or her half of the game board and then writes the compound word on the apple.
   e. If the two words *do not* form a compound word, the player places the leaf shapes facedown again.

f. Players take turns trying to find words that form compound words. The first player to find six word pairs that make compound words wins the game.

6. Turn over a pair of leaf cutouts, and ask students if they form a compound word. Do this several times to check that students understand how to play the game. Circulate around the room to monitor progress and answer questions as needed.

7. Close the activity by having each student name a new compound word that was not used in the game.

978-1-4129-5932-2

Compound Words

afternoon	carpool	jellyfish	sidewalk
airplane	classmate	lifeboat	snowball
airport	daydream	moonlight	starfish
applesauce	doghouse	notebook	strawberry
backbone	doorknob	outline	sunflower
backpack	driveway	pancake	tiptoe
backyard	earthworm	rainbow	tugboat
barefoot	fireplace	raincoat	upstairs
baseball	flashlight	rowboat	watercolor
bathroom	football	sailboat	waterfall
breakfast	goldfish	seashell	weekend
butterfly	haircut	seesaw	windmill
campfire	hotdog	shoelace	wristwatch

Extended Learning

- Have students play a game in the style of Pictionary® (a registered trademark of Pictionary Incorporated). Write compound words on index cards. Then have students select a card and draw a picture of each half of the compound word. For example, for *ponytail*, students would draw a picture of a pony and a tail.

- Invite students to write simple rebus sentences that include pictures of compound words.

978-1-4129-5932-2

An Apple a Day

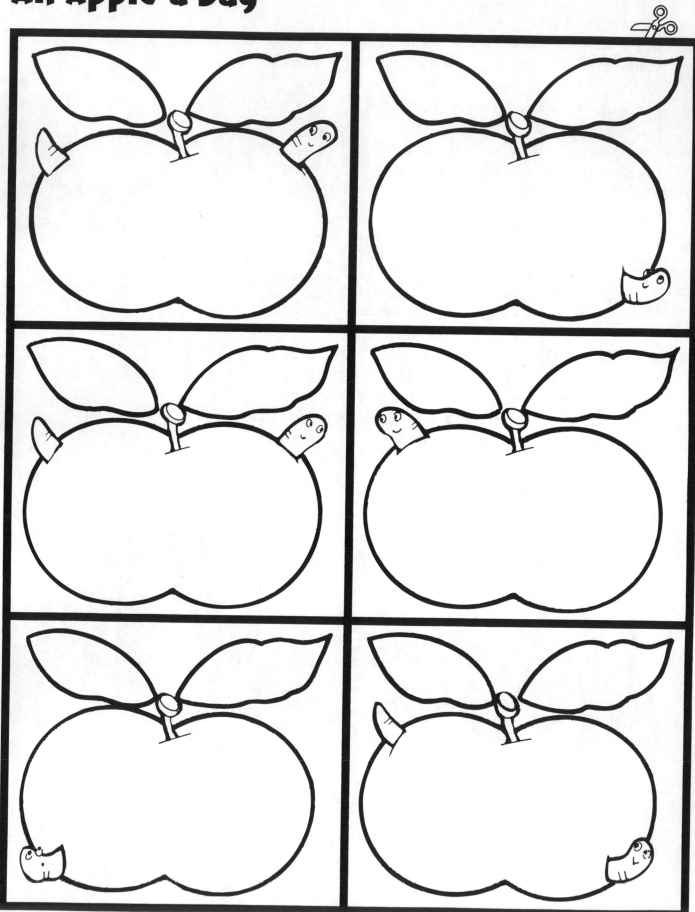

978-1-4129-5932-2 • © Corwin Press

pple Leaf Patterns

Name That Book

Materials

- pictures of book covers
- construction paper
- glue
- hole punch
- yarn

Objectives

Students will recall details and events from stories.
Students will ask and respond to questions.
Students will retell central ideas from stories.

In this game, students use deductive reasoning as they ask questions and gather clues that help them identify familiar stories. Who will solve the mystery before the questions run out?

1. Ahead of time, copy or print out images of covers from books that your class has read. You can find images on Web sites of online book retailers.

2. Mount each book cover picture on construction paper. Punch two holes in the top corners of the paper, thread yarn through the holes, and tie knots to create a "necklace." The yarn should make a loop long enough so the necklace can be worn safely around a student's neck.

3. Ask students about their favorite books. Encourage them to discuss the characters, settings, and plots of the books and what makes the books so enjoyable.

4. Select a book-cover necklace without looking at the picture. Put the loop of yarn over your head so the picture rests on your back. Turn around so the class can see the picture. Ask *yes* or *no* questions to get clues about the identity of the book. For example: *Is the main character in my book a person? Does the story take place a long time ago? Does the story take place in a school?* When you think you can identify the book, ask: *Is the title of my book _____?*

5. Tell students it is now their turn to play Name That Book. Explain that each pair of students will look at their partner's picture and take turns asking two *yes* or *no* questions each. If they cannot identify their books after two questions, they must move on to new partners. Ask students who have identified their books to sit at their desks until everyone has finished.

6. Model asking several questions to help students recognize the types of questions they should ask. For example: *Who is the main character in this book?* Have students suggest alternative questions with the correct format, such as: *Is this book about a girl?* Then have students stand in a circle with their backs to you. Place one necklace around each student's neck. Then begin the game.

7. As a follow-up, have students share their book cover and tell something about the story. Encourage them to tell about a favorite character or event.

Extended Learning

- Have students make simple puppets of the characters from their favorite books. Let them use the puppets to retell the stories.

- Ask students to write short paragraphs about the stories and then glue their writing on the backs of the necklaces.

- Encourage students to use Venn diagrams to compare and contrast two different book characters.

Super Synonyms

Materials
- Super Synonyms Scorecard reproducible
- cardstock
- paper clips
- brass fasteners
- picture books
- chart paper
- index cards

Objectives
Students will read aloud words and use the words in sentences. Students will identify synonyms for given words.

Students won't be bored with synonyms when they play with a board game they helped to create. Super Synonyms makes vocabulary practice super fun!

1. Ahead of time, cut circles out of cardstock to make game spinners. Make the circles about four to six inches in diameter. Divide the circles into thirds. Number the sections *1–3*. Attach paper clips to brass paper fasteners. Push one fastener through the center of each circle to make the spinner.

2. Motivate student interest in this game by enlisting their help in creating it. First, tell the class that a *synonym* is a word that has the same or similar meaning as another word. Use *pretty* as an example, and name some synonyms (e.g., *beautiful, lovely, gorgeous*). Then say *big* and ask volunteers to name synonyms for it (e.g., *huge, giant, large*). Tell students they will work in teams to list words with at least three synonyms. The words they choose will be used in the Super Synonyms game.

3. Divide the class into groups of four. Give each group a sheet of paper and a few familiar picture books. Tell students to look through the books to find words that have at least three synonyms. Have one student write the words on the paper. Ask group members to name synonyms for each word, and have the writer list them next to the original word. Have groups list synonyms for five words.

4. Invite groups to present their list to the class. Make a master list of the words and synonyms on a sheet of chart paper. For each word, ask if members of other groups can add more synonyms.

5. Then give each group 30 to 40 index cards. Tell groups to choose words from the master list and write one word on each card. These will be their game cards.

6. Next, give each group a game spinner, and give each player a copy of the **Super Synonyms Scorecard reproducible (page 24)**. Explain and model the rules of the game.
   a. One player shuffles the word cards and places them facedown in a stack.

b. The first player draws a card, reads aloud the word, and uses it in a sentence.

c. Next, the player spins the spinner. The number on which the paper clip stops tells the number of synonyms the player must name for the word on the card. For example, if the spinner lands on number *2* and the card has the word *small*, the player must name two synonyms, such as *tiny* and *little*.

d. If the player is able to name the correct number of synonyms, he or she colors the matching number of squares on the scorecard. If not, the player does nothing.

e. The next player then takes a turn.

f. To complete the scorecard, the player must spin the exact number needed to color in the remaining squares. For example, if there are only two squares left, the player cannot spin a 3.

g. The first player to color in all the squares on his or her scorecard wins the game.

7. Have each student take a practice turn to be sure everyone understands how to play. Then let groups play the game as you circulate around the room to monitor progress.

8. After the game, have volunteers select a word card, read aloud the word, and use it in two different sentences, substituting a synonym for the word in the second sentence.

Name _____ Date _____

Super Synonyms Scorecard

Directions: Pick a word card. Color one square for each synonym you name for the word.

Reproducible

Scrambled Sentences

Objectives
Students will arrange words to create complete and coherent sentences. Students will use basic rules of capitalization and punctuation in writing.

Will students "crack" under pressure or work together as a team? In this game, students test their grammar and punctuation skills as they unscramble sentences inside brightly-colored plastic eggs.

Materials
• plastic eggs
• empty egg cartons
• envelopes
• scissors
• tape

1. Ahead of time, write 12 sentences with which you want students to work. Include declarative, exclamatory, and interrogative sentences. Use contractions, proper nouns, and possessive nouns.

2. Type the sentences on a computer using a 36-point font. Use lowercase letters for all capital letters and do not include any punctuation. Here are a few samples:

   jeffs dog has brown spots   *im so surprised to see you*

   where is carlas book   *pam has a blue shirt*

3. Print enough copies of the sentences so you have one copy for every four students. Cut apart the words for each sentence and place them in a plastic egg. Fill one egg carton with 12 eggs for each group of four students.

4. Make an answer sheet that shows the words in the correct order with proper capitalization and punctuation. Print a copy for each team, place the paper in an envelope, and tape it to the inside lid of the egg carton.

5. Write a scrambled sentence on the board. Model how to put the words in the proper order, and correct any mistakes in capitalization and punctuation.

6. Divide the class into groups of four. Give each group one filled egg carton and a sheet of writing paper. Then explain and model the rules of the game.

   a. The game is played for ten minutes. The game starts at your signal.

   b. Each team chooses one player to be the writer.

   c. Team members work in pairs. Each pair opens an egg and takes out the word cards. Players arrange the words to form a complete sentence. Then partners identify and correct any capitalization and punctuation errors.

   d. The writer records the sentence on the writing paper, using correct word order, capitalization, and punctuation. Partners then choose another egg and unscramble a new sentence.

   e. At the end of ten minutes, signal that the game is over. Teams take their answer sheet out of the envelope to check their work. For every sentence teams have written correctly, they score one point.

   f. The team with the most points wins the game!

7. Write another scrambled sentence on the board. Have volunteers put the words in the correct order and identify any errors. Write the corrected sentence on the board. Then invite students to begin the game.

8. After the game, close the activity by having teams write one corrected sentence on the board. Have one student write the sentence and one student read it aloud. Ask other team members to identify the mistakes they corrected.

Extended Learning

- Make a Word Wall with words that begin with capital letters (proper nouns). Encourage students to add words each day.

- Write a declarative sentence on the board. Challenge students to rewrite the sentence as a question and then as an exclamation.

978-1-4129-5932-2

CHAPTER 2

Mathematics

Mystery Number Train

Objectives

Students will identify, count, read, and write numbers to 100. Students will count and group objects in ones and tens.

This game provides a new way to use the familiar 100 chart. Which student will put together the clues and be the first to identify the "mystery number"?

1. Ahead of time, decorate a bulletin board with a colorful train scene. Staple ten paper or plastic cups in a row for the train cars. Connect the train cars together with short lengths of yarn. Use tens to number the cars in order (e.g., *10, 20, 30*). Add a construction paper train engine and caboose.

2. Spark students' interest in the game by having them fill the "train cars" with straws, ten in each car.
   a. To begin, give a direction such as: *Stand up if you have at least one pet.*
   b. Tell all students standing to hold up their fingers to indicate how many pets they have.
   c. Count the number and write it on the board. If the number is greater than nine, point out how the tens place and ones place work together to make the whole number.

d. Allow these students to add a straw to a train car for each pet they have. Have them first fill the tens car with ten straws before moving on to the following cars.

e. Have volunteers use rubber bands to bind together each set of ten straws.

3. Continue giving directions, asking questions about favorite colors, number of family members, favorite school subjects, and so on, until each train car is filled with ten straws. Then have students count to 100 by tens.

4. Next, make several copies of **The Number Train reproducible (page 30)** for yourself and one copy for each student. On each of your copies, color in the boxes to create a "mystery number." Include both single-digit and double-digit numbers. See the grids below that show the numbers *7* and *32*.

5. Give students a copy of the reproducible and a handful of small paper squares. Choose one of the colored charts you made in Step 4. Then explain and model the rules of the game.

a. You will randomly call out a number in one of the colored boxes on the chart. You may choose to simply name a colored number or provide clues for it. For example, if the box for 56 is colored, call out *56* or use clues such as: *This number has six ones and five tens. This number is five more than 51.*

b. Students identify the number and cover it on their chart with a paper square. You also should cover or cross out the number to keep track of which numbers you have called.

c. As soon as a player can identity the mystery number, he or she raises a hand and makes a guess.

d. If the player is correct, he or she chooses a new colored chart for the next game. If the student is not correct, play continues until someone correctly identifies the number.

6. Play several practice rounds to check that students understand how to play. Then have them clear their charts and play a real game with you.

7. As a follow-up, have volunteers select a number on the 100 chart and give clues for the number until someone correctly identifies it.

Extended Learning

- Read counting books with students, such as *Let's Count* by Tana Hoban. Then encourage them to make their own counting books.

- Have students work in small groups to create posters that show 100 items. Display the posters with the train bulletin board.

The Number Train

1	2	3	4	5	6	7	8	9	10
11	12	13	14	15	16	17	18	19	20
21	22	23	24	25	26	27	28	29	30
31	32	33	34	35	36	37	38	39	40
41	42	43	44	45	46	47	48	49	50
51	52	53	54	55	56	57	58	59	60
61	62	63	64	65	66	67	68	69	70
71	72	73	74	75	76	77	78	79	80
81	82	83	84	85	86	87	88	89	90
91	92	93	94	95	96	97	98	99	100

Reproducible   978-1-4129-5932-2 • © Corwin Press

Fun Facts Bingo

Objective
Students will add numbers with sums up to 20 and complete the corresponding subtraction problems.

Materials
- Fun Facts Bingo Card reproducible
- index cards
- counters
- paper bag
- small paper squares
- overhead projector and transparency (optional)

Everyone wants to be the first to call out *Bingo!* This version of the favorite game gives students a fun way to practice multiple math skills as they identify and write numerals, solve addition and subtraction equations, use mental math, and commit math facts to memory.

1. Most students are familiar with the classic game of Bingo. To get students excited about playing this math-based version, ask them to share the different types of Bingo games they have played. Perhaps they have played the traditional version as well as versions that involve searching for pictures or words.

2. Next, choose a number from 0 to 20. Ask students to name addition problems whose sums equal the chosen number. Record each problem on a separate index card. For example, if the sum is six, record the following addition problems: *0 + 6, 1 + 5, 2 + 4, 3 + 3, 4 + 2, 5 + 1, 6 + 0.*

3. Have students identify subtraction problems whose differences equal the chosen number. (For subtraction problems, 20 should be the largest minuend used.) Record each problem on a separate index card. If the chosen number is six, record the following subtraction problems: *6 − 0, 7 − 1, 8 − 2, 9 − 3, 10 − 4, 11 − 5, 12 − 6, 13 − 7, 14 − 8, 15 − 9, 16 − 10, 17 − 11, 18 − 12, 19 − 13, 20 − 14.*

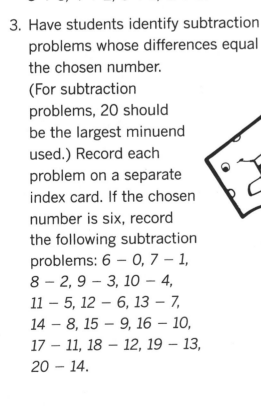

4. Have students prepare more index cards for the math Bingo game. Then divide the class into small groups. Assign each group one or two numbers from 0 to 20. Have students work together to record the addition and subtraction problems for their assigned numbers, just as you did in Steps 2 and 3. Provide counters for students who need them. Gather the completed game cards and place them in a bag.

5. Give students a copy of the **Fun Facts Bingo Card reproducible (page 34)**. Tell them to write numbers from *0* to *20* in the squares on the Bingo card. The numbers can be arranged in any order they wish, and some numbers will need to be repeated. Display an overhead transparency of the reproducible and model this step if you wish.

6. Give students some paper squares to use as game markers. Draw an index card from the bag, read aloud the problem; and ask students to identify the answer. Have them look for this number on their game card. If they have the number, they should cover it with a paper square. They should only cover one number at a time. Read aloud several more problems, and ask volunteers to give the answers to check for understanding.

7. Make sure everyone understands how to play, and then begin the game by drawing another index card and reading aloud the problem. Keep track of the answers as you go. The first player to cover five squares in a row calls out: *Bingo!* Have that student read aloud the numbers he or she covered. If the numbers in the row are the answers to the math problems you read, the student wins the game.

8. Play several rounds of the game, but vary the requirements for winning. For example, in one round the first player to cover all 25 squares on the game card wins. In another round, the first player to cover all four corners of the game card wins.

Extended Learning

- Use the index cards you prepared for the Bingo game as part of a Math Bee. Divide the class into two teams, and have each team stand in a single-file line. Show a math problem to the first player on each team. The first player to solve the problem scores a point for his or her team.

- Encourage students to use number lines to identify one more than, one less than, ten more than, and ten less than a given number.

Fun Facts Bingo Card

F	A	C	T	S
		FREE **SPACE**		

"Keep the Change" Go Fish

Objectives
Students will identify and learn the value of coins.
Students will show different coin combinations that have the same value.

Students will enjoy playing a game of Go Fish using cards they helped to make. They won't even realize they're practicing essential math skills as they play!

1. Get students warmed up for this activity by allowing them to explore and play with some coins. Call out a value, such as *ten cents*. Challenge students to come up with as many ways as possible to show that value. Let one student at a time describe a set of coins that equal that value. Challenge students to think of as many different sets as possible.

2. Divide the class into groups of four. Give each group 64 index cards, and instruct them to divide the cards evenly among themselves. To keep the card sets organized, you may wish to give each group a different-colored set of cards.

3. Ask each group member to choose four different coin values, ranging from ten cents to 99 cents. Encourage group members to share with each other which values they select so no values are repeated.

Materials
- plastic coins (quarters, dimes, nickels, pennies)
- index cards
- rubber stamps of a quarter, dime, nickel, and penny
- stamp pads
- chart paper

4. Next, give each group a stamp pad and a set of rubber stamps showing a quarter, a dime, a nickel, and a penny. Have students use the stamps to show four different coin combinations for each value they chose. (Each student creates 16 game cards.) Demonstrate how to do this by stamping four index cards with coin combinations that total ten cents. For example, stamp the first card with a dime, the second with two nickels, the third with ten pennies, and the fourth with one nickel and five pennies.

5. Explain that students will play a variation of the card game *Go Fish*. The object of the game is to collect sets of cards that show the same coin values. A complete set will have four cards. Have groups shuffle the cards and deal seven cards facedown to each player. Tell them to place the rest of the cards facedown in a draw pile.

6. Have one group deal a set of cards to you so you can model how to play the game.
   a. Players organize their cards so that like cards are next to each other. Use the cards in your hand to demonstrate.
   b. Players pull out any complete sets of four and place the sets faceup in front of them.
   c. Player 1 chooses a card from his or her hand, such as a card showing 48 cents. Player 1 asks Player 2: *Do you have 48 cents?* Player 2 must give Player 1 any cards in his or her hand that show a coin combination with a value of 48 cents.
   d. If Player 1 is able to collect any cards from Player 2, he or she gets another turn. If Player 2 does not have a card showing 48 cents, he or she says: *Go fish.* Then Player 1 must draw one card from the draw pile, and Player 2 gets a turn.
   e. Each time a complete set is made, that player places the cards faceup on the table.
   f. The game is over when all 16 sets of cards have been found and placed together in sets. The winner is the player who has the most sets.
   g. If players run out of cards in their hand before the end of the game, they must draw three cards from the draw pile on their next turn.

7. Check that students understand how to play the game. Then let them play in their groups. Circulate among students and assist as needed.

8. Close the activity by allowing groups to share the coin values they chose and how they represented them.

Extended Learning

- Set up a mock store in the classroom. Let students take turns working and shopping in the store. Have them label the items with prices and use plastic coins to "buy" the items.

- Have students look through newspaper grocery ads and count out coins to show how much different items cost.

Time's Up! Beanbag Toss

Objective
Students will tell time to the nearest half-hour.

Materials
• Time's Up! Game Cards reproducibles
• scissors
• paper lunch bags
• chalk
• beanbags

A beanbag toss game is an engaging way for students to practice math skills. In this activity, students identify times shown on analog clocks and then toss beanbags onto a target showing the same times in a digital format.

1. Ahead of time, make a copy of the **Time's Up! Game Cards reproducibles (pages 41–42)** for each group of four students. Cut out the clock cards, and place one set of cards in a paper bag for each group.

2. Use chalk to draw a bull's-eye diagram on the playground for each group. (See the diagram below.) Draw a line about two yards away from the bull's-eye to show where students should stand during the game. Enlist the help of teacher's aides, assistants, or parent volunteers if needed.

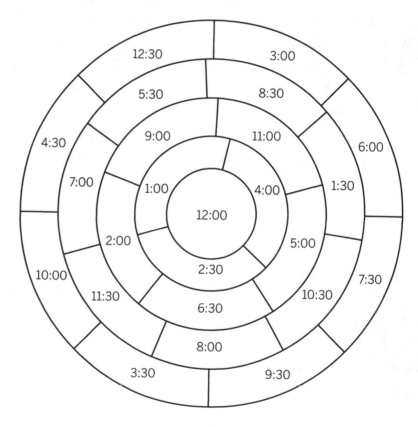

3. Take the class outside, and have students line up in a row. Give each student a beanbag. Have students toss their beanbags and determine who threw the farthest. Then point out several different targets, some nearby and others a little farther away. See who can get his or her beanbag closest to the target.

4. Divide the class into groups of four. Assign each group a bull's-eye, and have group members use chalk to write their names nearby. Explain that they will use tally marks to record points next to their names. Give each group three beanbags and a paper bag filled with clock cards.

5. Explain and model the rules of the game.
   a. The first player draws a clock card from the bag and reads aloud the time shown on the clock.
   b. Then the player finds the matching time on the bull's-eye and tries to toss the beanbags so they land on that space.
   c. To score points, one or more beanbags must land in the spacc that matches the time shown on the clock card. If a beanbag lands on a line, it does not score any points.
   d. There are five rings in the bull's-eye. The center circle is worth five points. Moving out from the center, each ring, in order, is worth four points, three points, two points, and one point.
   e. After the player tosses all three beanbags, he or she adds up the points earned and records the score.
   f. Players take turns drawing clock cards and tossing beanbags.
   g. The first player to earn 15 points wins the game!

6. Have each student take one practice turn to make sure everyone understands how to play. Then let groups begin their games. Help students in recording and adding their scores, if needed.

7. Close the activity by asking questions related to students' scores. For example: *How many more points does Mina have than Nolan? To get to 15, how many more points would Jessie need?*

Extended Learning

- Have students make mini-books showing the times of day when different activities are typically done. For example, a student might write: *I wake up at 6:30. I eat breakfast at 7:00. I go to soccer practice at 3:00.*

- Have students keep track of the amount of time they spend each day doing different activities (e.g., reading, exercising, eating). Help them graph the results.

Time's Up! Game Cards

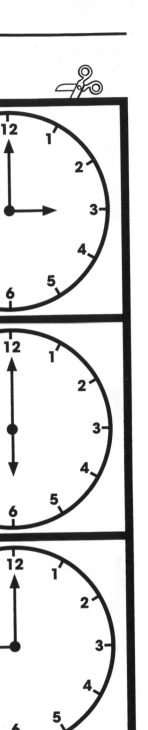

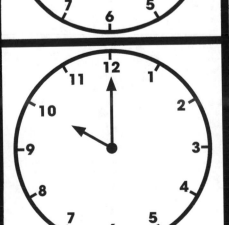

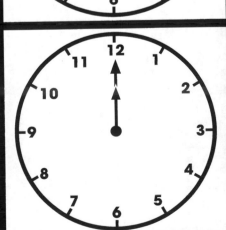

Time's Up! Game Cards

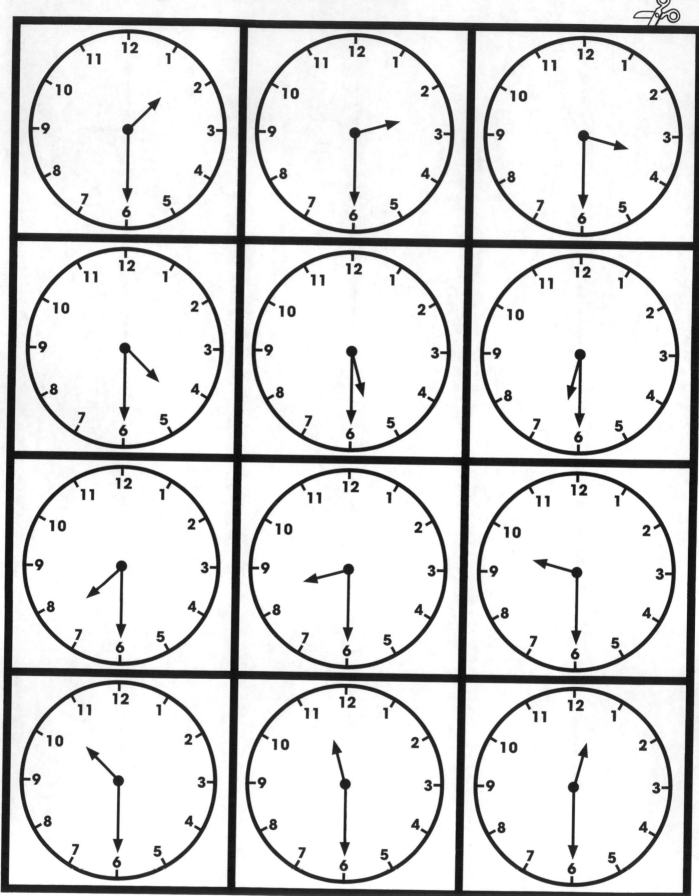

978-1-4129-5932-2 • © *Corwin Press*

Tricky Tangrams

Objective
Students will use rotations and flips to make images with geometric shapes.

Students' experiences with jigsaw puzzles will help form the foundation for this activity. Like jigsaw puzzles, tangrams involve combining shapes to create a given image. In this "puzzling" game, students will rotate and flip pieces, putting them together and taking them apart to create various animals.

1. Ahead of time, copy the **Tangram Puzzle Pieces reproducible (page 45)** on colored cardstock for each student and for yourself. Cut out the puzzle pieces, and place each set in a plastic bag (one bag for each student pair). Then copy the **Puzzling Puzzles reproducibles (pages 46–47)** on cardstock for each student. Make double-sided copies so the puzzles are on one side and the solutions are on the other. Cut out the boxes to create six puzzle cards.

2. Give each student pair a bag of puzzle pieces. Let students spend some time experimenting with the "tans" (shapes) to see what images they can create. Invite volunteers to share their images by placing them on an overhead projector.

3. Give each student pair a set of Puzzling Puzzles cards. Students will use these cards and the tangram puzzle pieces in the game.

4. Explain the rules of playing with tangrams.
   a. All seven tans (shapes) must be used to make an image.
   b. The tans must lay flat and cannot overlap.
   c. Every tan must touch at least one other tan.

5. Use an overhead projector to model how to use the tans to make an image. Then explain the rules of the game.
   a. Players place their Puzzling Puzzles cards in a stack with the silhouette images showing.
   b. They look at the top card and use their tans to try to replicate the image.
   c. The first player to correctly match the image keeps the puzzle card. Then the players try to replicate the image shown on the next card.
   d. If players cannot solve the puzzle, they may look at the solution on the back of the card. Players use their tans to copy the solution and then place the card in a discard pile.
   e. The game is over when all the puzzle cards have been collected or discarded. The player with the most cards wins.

6. Make sure students understand how to play the game by having them play one practice round. As they play, circulate around the room to offer guidance and answer questions.

7. Close the activity by having volunteers demonstrate the solution for each puzzle on the overhead projector.

Extended Learning

- Have students write short stories about one or more of the animals shown on the Puzzling Puzzles cards. Encourage students to use their tans to illustrate the stories.

- Invite students to create their own tangram picture puzzles. Challenge them to solve each other's puzzles.

T_ngram Puzzle Pieces

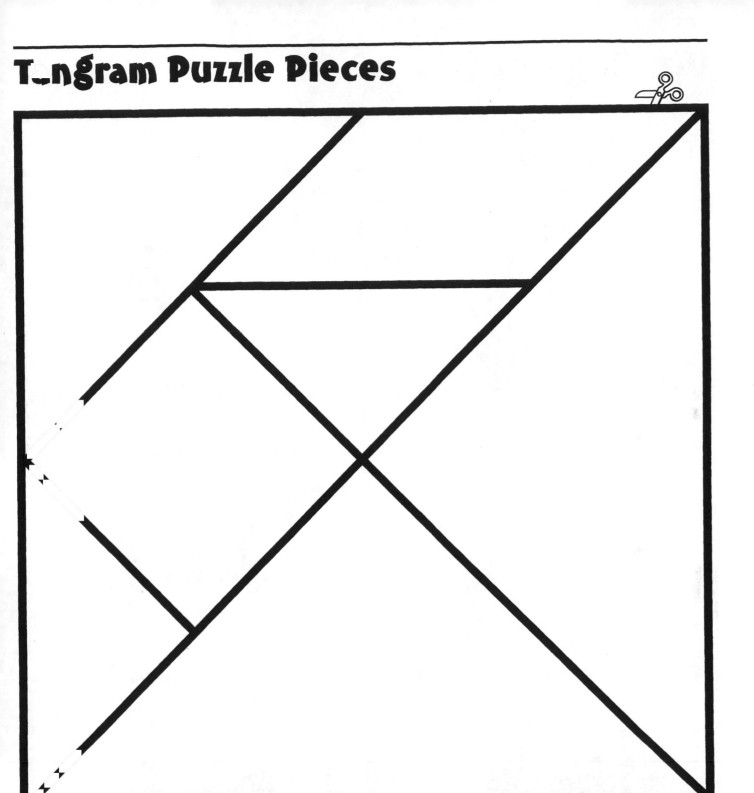

Puzzling Puzzles

Images created by Randy Crawford, *www.tangrams.ca*. Used with permission.

978-1-4129-5932-2 • © Corwin Press

Puzzling Puzzles: Solutions

Images created by Randy Crawford, *www.tangrams.ca*. Used with permission.

CHAPTER 3

Science

"Mind Over Matter" Relay Race

Materials
- block of wood
- glass of water
- clear balloon
- 12 index cards per team
- old magazines, stickers, stamps
- crayons or markers
- scissors
- glue
- shoe boxes
- chart paper
- tape

Objectives

Students will learn that matter comes in different forms, including solids, liquids, and gases.

Students will sort matter into categories of solids, liquids, and gases.

In this exciting game, students compete in a relay race as they demonstrate their knowledge of solids, liquids, and gases. Which team can sort its picture cards into the proper categories the fastest? Mind Over Matter is one solid game!

1. Display a block of wood, a glass of water, and a clear, uninflated balloon. Ask students: *Which object is a solid?* (wood) Ask for other examples of solid materials. Continue with the glass of water and liquids. Then, inflate the balloon. Ask what kind of matter you put into the balloon when you blew it up. *(air)* Ask: *Is air a solid, liquid, or gas?* (gas) Ask for other examples of gases.

2. Next, divide the class into teams of four. Give each team 12 index cards, old magazines, stickers, stamps, crayons or markers, scissors, and glue. Tell students they will glue pictures of solids, liquids, and gases to the cards. They must have at least three pictures of each type of matter. Give suggestions for gases (e.g., steam from a tea kettle, air as shown in a blue sky, helium in a balloon, smoke from a fire, bubbles in a fizzy drink). Tell students that they can use the materials you've given them for their pictures, or they can draw and label their own pictures.

tree   rain   steam

3. Prepare a set of three shoe boxes for each team while students are making their cards. Label the boxes *Solids, Liquids,* and *Gases.*

4. Take the class to a playing field, and have teams line up single file. Place the boxes some distance away from the teams. Place each team's picture cards in a stack in front of their boxes.

5. Tell students that they will race to see which team can sort their picture cards the fastest. Model for students how to run the relay race.
   a. The first player runs to the stack of cards.
   b. The player picks up the first card, identifies the picture, and places the card in the correct box.
   c. He or she then runs back to the team and tags the next player in line.
   d. The first team to sort all of its picture cards correctly wins the game.

6. Display several picture cards from different teams, and ask students to identify each picture and tell in which box it belongs. Be sure students understand what to do, and then start the race.

7. Close the activity by having each team share its picture cards with the class and identify the pictures that show solids, liquids, and gases. Tape the cards in three columns on chart paper to create a class chart.

"Plant Power" Board Game

Materials

- Parts of a Plant reproducible
- Plant Power Game Cards reproducible
- overhead projector and transparency
- samples of edible plants (e.g., apples, celery, carrots, broccoli, lettuce)
- seed catalogs
- scissors
- glue
- butcher paper
- crayons or markers
- game markers (e.g., small paper squares, pennies, counters)

Objectives

Students will identify the parts of a plant.
Students will identify which part of a given edible plant is the part that is eaten.

In this board game, students match pictures of plant parts to pictures of plants that are used for food. Students start the game in the "garden" and move their game markers along the path until they reach the "table." The first player to get to the table wins the game!

1. Display a transparency of the **Parts of a Plant reproducible (page 53)**. Use it to show students that plants have roots, a stem, leaves, flowers, and fruit.

2. Display a collection of edible plants, such as apples, celery, carrots, broccoli, and lettuce. The foods should be as close to their natural state as possible. Help students name the foods. Then challenge them to identify which part of the plant we actually eat (e.g., *apple—fruit; celery—stem; carrots—roots; broccoli—flowers; lettuce—leaves*).

3. Divide the class into small groups. Give each group a seed catalog. Seed catalogs can be ordered online through Web sites such as *www.burpee.com* and *www.parkseed.com*. Have students cut out pictures of edible plants from the catalogs.

4. Then have them sort the pictures based on what part of the plant is eaten—fruit, stem, roots, flowers, or leaves. Have each group collect 20 to 25 pictures showing some plants from each category. Display a chart like that on page 51 to help students sort. Include pictures of the plants.

Fruit	Stem	Roots	Flowers	Leaves
apple	asparagus	beet	cauliflower	lettuce
orange	celery	turnip	broccoli	spinach
squash	green onion	carrot	sunflower	arugula
cucumber	water chestnut	jicama	brussels sprout	basil
plum		potato	artichoke	cilantro

5. Have groups glue their pictures on sheets of paper, fitting as many pictures as they can on each page. Collect the picture pages from each group. Have a teacher's aide or assistant make several copies of each page.

6. Give each group its set of photocopied pages. Have students cut out the pictures. Tell them they will use these pieces to create their game boards.

7. Give each group a three-foot-long strip of butcher paper. Tell students to draw a garden scene on one end of the paper and a table on the opposite end. Have them mix up their plant pictures and arrange them in a path between the garden and the table. The path should wind around the paper. Instruct students to glue the pictures in place, and draw arrows showing the direction the path travels.

8. While students are building their game boards, make three copies of the **Plant Power Game Cards reproducible (page 54)** for each team. Cut out the cards.

9. Then explain and model how to play the game.
   a. Each player selects a game marker, while one player shuffles the game cards and places them facedown in a stack.
   b. The first player draws a card and identifies the part of a plant shown. Then he or she finds the first plant on the game board with a matching edible part. For example, if the player has a leaf card, he or she looks for a plant with edible leaves, such as lettuce or spinach.
   c. The player moves his or her marker to the appropriate spot on the game board, and the next player takes a turn.
   d. Play continues as players follow the arrows to move along the path on the game board.
   e. The first player to move his or her marker from the garden to the table wins.

10. Have each student take one practice turn to make sure everyone understands how to play. Then invite groups to play the game.

11. As a follow-up, ask volunteers to compare and contrast the characteristics of two different plants from the game boards.

Extended Learning

- Encourage students to write recipes for dishes that include edible plants. Combine the recipes to make a class cookbook.

- Have students conduct taste tests for different edible plants. Ask students to name their favorites, and have them use the results to create a class graph.

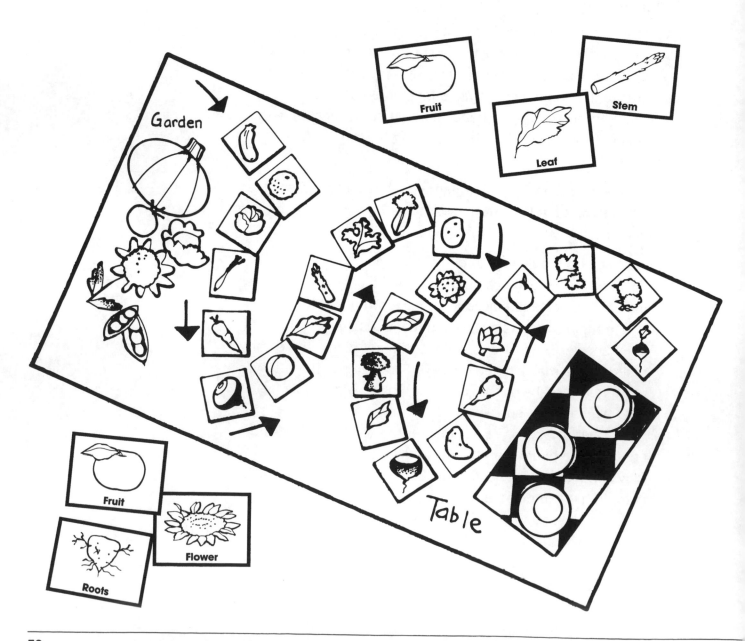

978-1-4129-5932-2

Parts of a Plant

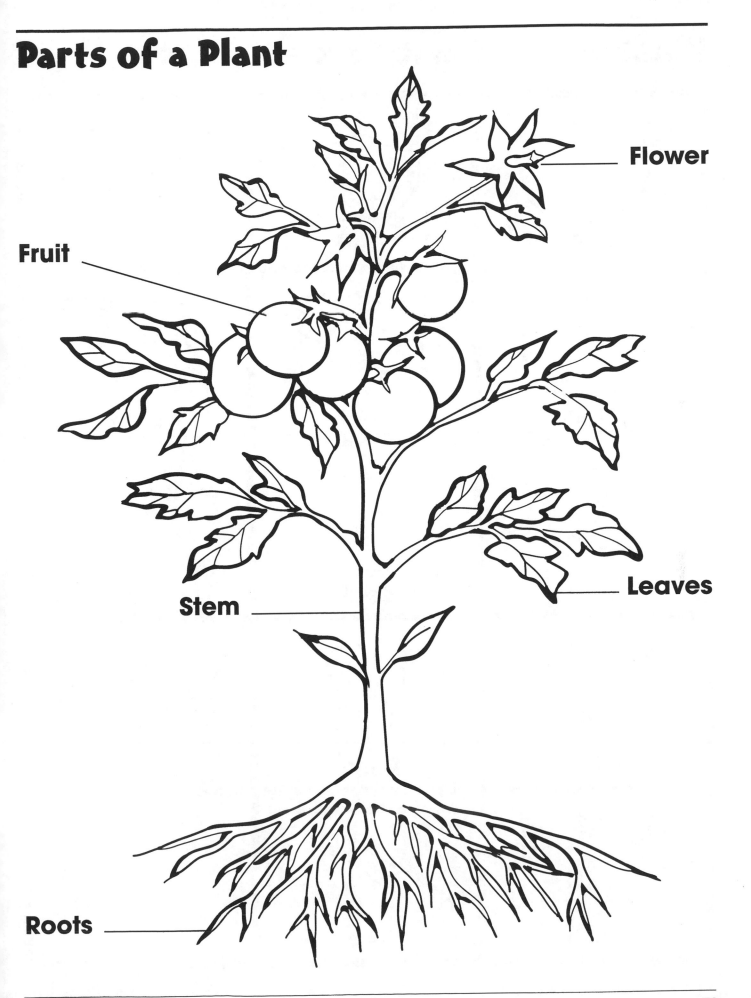

Flower

Fruit

Leaves

Stem

Roots

Plant Power Game Cards

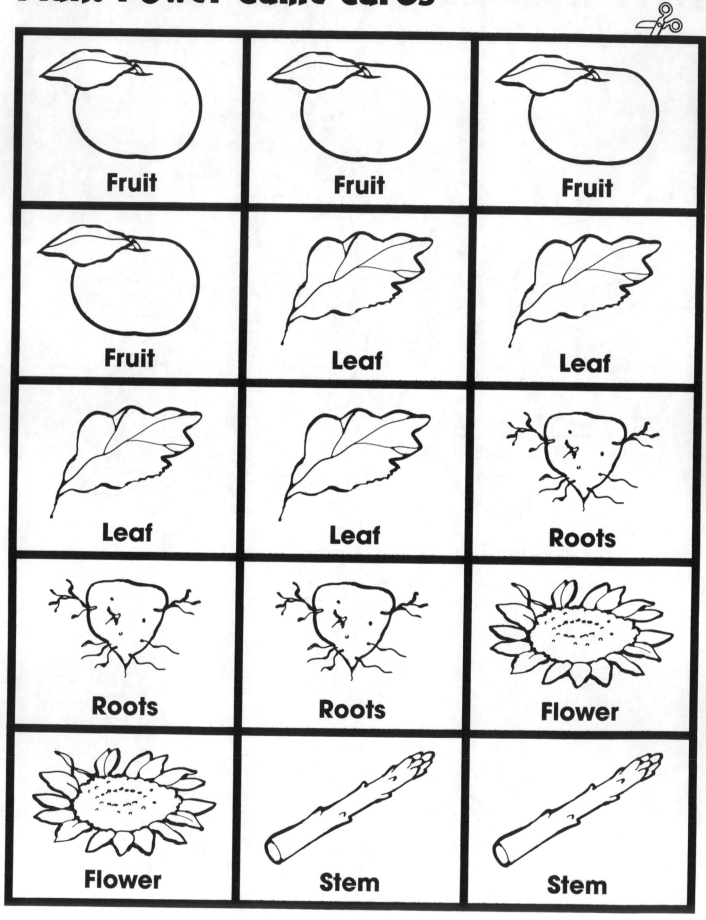

Fruit

Fruit

Fruit

Fruit

Leaf

Leaf

Leaf

Leaf

Roots

Roots

Roots

Flower

Flower

Stem

Stem

978-1-4129-5932-2 • © Corwin Press

"Happy Homes" Quiz Game

Objectives
Students will identify different types of environments.
Students will describe plants and animals that live in given environments.

Materials
• books and posters about different environments
• chart paper
• markers
• index cards
• overhead projector and transparency
• signaling device (e.g., bell, drum)
• butcher paper
• art supplies

Students love to show off what they know. Let your young contestants shine in this quiz game as they use what they know about environments to score points for their team.

1. Ask students to tell about games they have watched on TV. Encourage them to describe how each game is played. Then tell them that they will help you make a quiz game about different environments.

2. Display books and posters about five different environments that the class has studied or is familiar with. Give students some time to peruse the materials independently. Then let them choose which environment they want to learn more about and form groups based on personal interests. You may wish to set a limit for the number of students in each group.

3. Tell groups that they will work together to write questions about their chosen environments. Model how to do this with an environment that was not among the choices. For example, you might choose *desert* and list questions on the board, such as: *What is a hill of sand piled up by the wind called?* (sand dune) *Why does a cactus have sharp spines?* (to protect it from hungry animals) Invite volunteers to suggest questions for your list.

4. Give each group a sheet of chart paper and a marker. Have students work together to brainstorm a list of at least ten questions for their environment. Have one person record the group's questions on the chart paper. At the end of the brainstorming session, instruct groups to circle their five best questions.

5. Collect the lists and copy the circled questions onto separate index cards. Assign each question a point value from 10 to 50, and label the index cards accordingly. Sort the cards into stacks so each environment has five cards, ordered by point value.

6. Draw a game board on the board. There should be five columns and six rows. Label each column with the name of an environment the class has studied.

7. Give each group a signaling device such as a bell or drum. Then explain the rules of the game.
   a. One team selects an environment and a point value. You will read aloud the appropriate question. The first team to signal will get a chance to answer the question.
   b. If they answer correctly, the team earns the number of points assigned to the question. If the answer is incorrect, another team may signal that they want to answer the question.
   c. Keep track of the score on the board.
   d. Play continues until all the questions have been answered. The team with the most points wins the game.

8. Choose a few questions that you did not use in making the index cards. Use the questions to play a practice round. Once you are sure everyone understands the game, begin a real game. Cross out the squares as students select categories and point values.

9. Close the activity by inviting groups to make murals of their environments. Provide butcher paper and art supplies. Use the murals for a classroom display.

978-1-4129-5932-2

Extended Learning

- Have students use a Venn diagram to compare and contrast two animals that live in the same environment, or compare and contrast two different environments.

- Have students print out pictures of plants and animals from the Internet. Challenge them to identify in which environment the plants and animals belong and add the pictures to the corresponding class murals.

Oceans	Forests	Wetlands	Mountains	Grasslands
X̶1̶0̶	10	10	10	
X̶2̶0̶	20	20	20	
30	30	30	X̶3̶0̶	
40	40	40	4	
50	50	50	50	

"Sensational Seasons" Guessing Game

Materials
- Sensational Seasons reproducible
- pictures of seasonal activities
- construction paper
- glue
- sand timer

Objectives
Students will describe activities appropriate for different seasons. Students will understand that weather changes from day to day, but seasonal trends are predictable.

This game challenges students to describe pictures of activities while avoiding using certain "forbidden" words. For example, try to describe flying a kite without using the words *kite*, *wind*, and *string*. Students will have to stretch their brains to find creative ways to describe familiar things if they want to win.

1. Ahead of time, collect a variety of pictures that show activities from each of the four seasons. Calendars, nature and travel magazines, and the Internet are all good sources. You can also invite families to donate photographs from family vacations or special events. If possible, collect at least 100 pictures.

2. Mount each picture on construction paper. At the top of the paper, write a title for the image, such as *Playing Basketball* or *Making Sand Castles*. Then, on a side margin, write three words that *cannot* be used to describe the activity. For example, for *Playing Basketball* you might choose the words *basketball*, *hoop*, and *jump*, and for *Making Sand Castles* you might choose *sand*, *beach*, and *bucket*.

978-1-4129-5932-2

3. Prepare students for playing this game by discussing the four seasons. Ask them to describe what the weather is like during winter, spring, summer, and fall. Then have students brainstorm a list of activities for each season. Record their ideas on the board.

4. Next, tell students that you are going to play a word game about weather and seasons. Divide the class into four teams. Give each team one copy of the **Sensational Seasons reproducible (page 61)**. Have teams choose a team name and write it on their paper.

5. Show students one of the picture cards. Point out the title at the top and the three forbidden words on the side. Explain that the object of the game is to get your team to guess the name of the activity without using any of the forbidden words.

6. Use the picture card to model how to play the game.
    a. A player from one team stands at the front of the room. The player chooses a picture card and looks at it without showing the picture to anyone. Then he or she silently reads the forbidden words on the side and the title at the top.
    b. The other teams each send one player to the front of the room. Those players get to see the picture and read the words. They stand silently next to the player with the picture card.
    c. Turn over the sand timer. The player with the picture card uses words to describe it. He or she cannot use any of the forbidden words or any gestures or actions.
    d. If the player uses one of the forbidden words on the card, the players from the other teams call out: *Stop!* Check the card. If a forbidden word was used, the turn is over and the team scores no points.
    e. If the team correctly guesses the activity before time runs out, they score one point. Then they color in one band of the rainbow on their scorecard.
    f. The title of the picture does not have to be named exactly as it is written. The goal is to identify the activity. If there is a question about whether or not the activity was correctly identified, you are the final judge.
    g. The first team to color all the bands of their rainbow wins the game.

7. Allow each team to play one practice round before starting the game. Ensure that everyone understands how to play, and then monitor the progress of the game.

8. After the game, have students sort the picture cards by the seasons they represent. Some pictures may represent more than one season. Then have each team choose a season and tell the class what the weather is typically like in your area during that season.

Extended Learning

• Have students use the picture cards to play charades. Rather than using words to describe the pictures, they must use only gestures and actions.

• Have each student choose a picture card and write a story about it. Encourage students to use descriptive, sensory language in their stories. Compile the stories in a class book.

Name _____ Date _____

Sensational Seasons

Directions: Color one band of the rainbow for each point your team scores.

_____

Team Name: _____

CHAPTER 4

Social Studies

"Symbols and Landmarks" Memory Match

Materials

- Symbols and Landmarks reproducibles
- scissors
- crayons or markers
- glue
- 8 1/2" x 11" construction paper, cut in half
- hole punch
- yarn

Objectives

Students will identify American symbols and landmarks.
Students will describe the people or events associated with American symbols and landmarks.

Test students' memories as well as their knowledge of important United States symbols and landmarks. Use this interactive game as a way to spark discussion, provide extended learning opportunities, and create mini-books.

1. Spark students' interest by asking them to help you make a game about United State symbols and landmarks. Give students a copy of the **Symbols and Landmarks reproducibles (pages 64–65)**. Have them cut out the cards and color the pictures. Then show them how to glue each picture to the top part of a construction paper square. After the game, students will add text at the bottom of each square, so it is important that the pictures are positioned correctly.

2. Discuss the pictures with the class. Ask volunteers to share any information they know about the symbols and landmarks. Encourage students to discuss why they are important to our country.

3. Next, divide the class into pairs, and have partners combine their picture cards. Model and explain the rules of the game.

    a. Partners have 16 pairs of picture cards. One player shuffles the cards and then places them facedown in four rows. There should be eight cards in each row.

    b. The first player turns over two cards. If the pictures match, the player keeps the cards and takes another turn. If the pictures do not match, the player places them facedown in their original positions.

    c. The next player then takes a turn.

    d. Play continues until all the matches have been found. The player with the most pairs wins.

4. Model playing several hands with a volunteer. Emphasize to students that the challenge of this game is to try and remember where they have seen cards before so they can use them to make matches later. Then have students play on their own.

5. After the game, have players sort their cards again so that each player has his or her original set of pictures. Then have students stack their picture cards faceup in numerical order. Punch two holes on the left-hand side of the cards, and use yarn to bind the cards together to make mini-books. Each day, choose one symbol or landmark to study in more detail. Help students locate information in books, in magazines, and on the Internet. Then have students write one or two sentences on the bottom of the corresponding picture card.

Extended Learning

- Have students make shoe-box dioramas that depict a national symbol or landmark from the picture cards.

- Display a large map of the United States on a bulletin board. Cut out the landmark cards on the Symbols and Landmarks reproducibles. Ask students to help you attach the pictures to the map to show where each landmark is located.

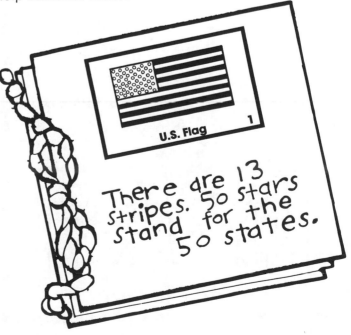

U.S. Flag   1

There are 13 stripes. 50 stars stand for the 50 states.

Symbols and Landmarks

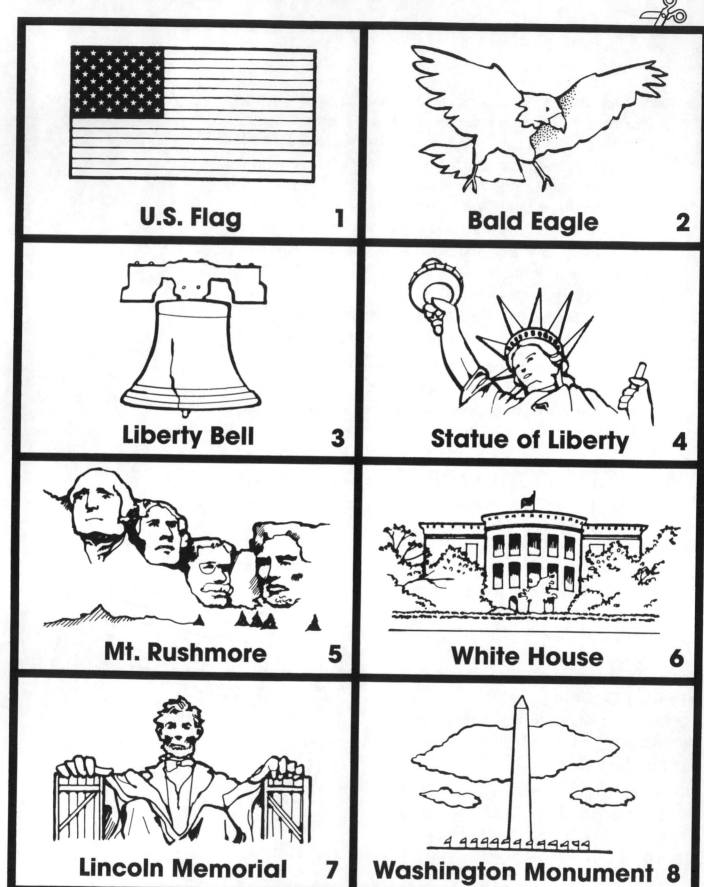

U.S. Flag 1

Bald Eagle 2

Liberty Bell 3

Statue of Liberty 4

Mt. Rushmore 5

White House 6

Lincoln Memorial 7

Washington Monument 8

978-1-4129-5932-2 • © Corwin Press

Symbols and Landmarks

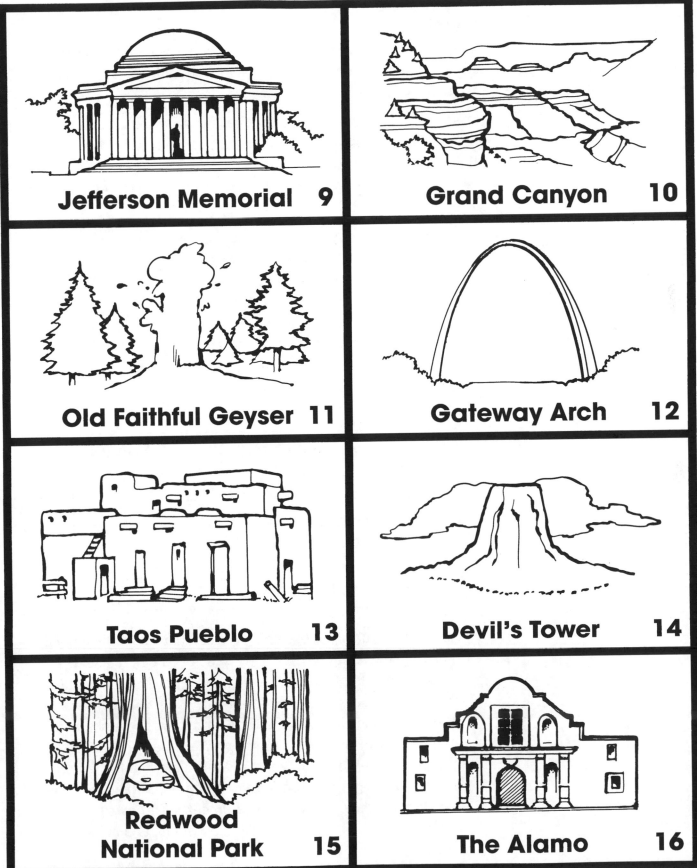

Jefferson Memorial 9

Grand Canyon 10

Old Faithful Geyser 11

Gateway Arch 12

Taos Pueblo 13

Devil's Tower 14

Redwood National Park 15

The Alamo 16

"Family Tree" Board Game

Materials

- "Family Tree" Game Board reproducible
- picture books about various cultures
- chart paper
- scissors
- glue sticks
- large index cards
- large resealable plastic bags
- green crayons

Objectives

Students will recognize various cultures within their communities. Students will compare the beliefs, customs, traditions, and social practices among different cultures.

Using children's literature is an excellent way to teach students about the many different cultures that contribute to American society. In this game, students will read several books about families from different cultures and then use what they learn to play a question-and-answer game.

1. Prepare students for the game by reading aloud six books that depict families from different cultures. See the book list for suggestions. The books on the list represent the following cultures: Hispanic, Chinese, Japanese, Greek, Native American, and African American. Choose one book to read aloud each day. After the reading, discuss with students the culture that was represented. Ask them to describe any beliefs, customs, traditions, or social practices that were evident in the book. List their ideas on chart paper.

> ### Books About Families from Different Cultures
> *Abuela* by Arthur Dorros
> *Grandfather Counts* by Andrea Cheng
> *Grandfather's Journey* by Allen Say
> *I Have an Olive Tree* by Eve Bunting
> *Morning on the Lake* by Jan Bourdeau Waboose
> *Tar Beach* by Faith Ringgold

2. After reading all six books, tell students that they will help you make a game about the books. Choose one book to use as a model. Read aloud the book again, and then challenge students to generate at least ten questions about it. Encourage them to incorporate questions that deal specifically with the characters' culture. For Eve Bunting's *I Have an Olive Tree*, for example, questions might include: *Where is Sofia's grandfather from?* (Greece) *What gift does Sofia's grandfather give her?* (an olive tree) *What is the name of the instrument Sofia hears being played at the dock?* (the bouzouki) List the questions and answers on chart paper.

3. Divide the class into five groups. Assign each group one of the remaining picture books, and have students list ten questions for the book. Enlist the help of a teaching assistant or parent to help each group type their questions and answers on a computer, listing the book's title and author above each question. Have groups put about five spaces between each question and print five copies of their work. Do the same for the book you worked on together as a class.

4. Next, tell students to cut apart their question sheets and glue each question and answer to a large index card. The index cards should have the title and author of the book at the top. Do the same for the questions you created. Ask groups to organize their cards into five stacks, with each stack containing all ten questions.

5. Collect all the index cards. Place a complete set of cards for each book in a large plastic bag. Each bag should contain 60 cards, ten cards for each book. Prepare a total of five bags.

6. Divide the class into ten teams, and invite students to think of a name for their team. Give teams a copy of the **"Family Tree" Game Board reproducible (page 69)** and a green crayon. Tell teams to write the title and author of each book on a separate tree branch.

7. Pair up each team with a partner team to play the game. Give each pair of teams one bag of question cards. Model and explain the rules of the game.

   a. One player shuffles the cards and places them facedown in a stack.

   b. One team draws a card and reads the book title, the author's name, and the question to the opposing team. The players on that team work together to answer the question.

   c. If the team answers the question correctly, they draw a leaf on the tree branch for that book on their game board. If they answer incorrectly, play passes to the other team.

   d. Teams take turns asking and answering questions.

   e. The first team to draw three leaves on the branch for each book wins the game.

8. At the end of the game, have students tell one new thing they learned about another culture.

Extended Learning

- Host a Culture Day in your classroom. Invite students to bring in food, traditional clothing, photographs, and other artifacts that represent their families' cultures. Ask students to present their artifacts to the class and tell about their cultures or special family traditions.

- Invite students to learn more about the cultures represented by the books you shared. Have students make posters, write stories, or sing songs for the cultures they choose to study.

Team Name _____ Date _____

"Family Tree" Game Board

Directions: Write the name of a book title and its author on each tree branch. Answer questions about the books before drawing leaves.

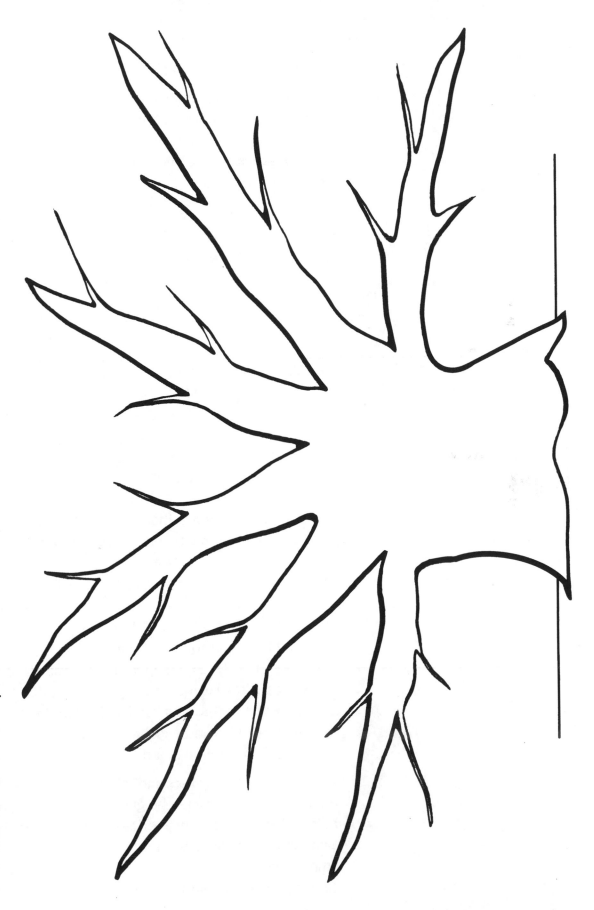

"Secrets to Citizenship" Telephone

Objective
Students will list examples of good citizenship.

In this classic game, students can enjoy a little silliness as they discuss the rights and responsibilities of citizenship. They will work together to write descriptions of good citizens. Then one student whispers a description to another student until everyone has heard it. Will the message change as it makes its way down the telephone line?

1. Show students a picture of an old-fashioned telephone. Point out how the receiver and mouthpiece are separate and that the receiver is attached to the box with a cord.

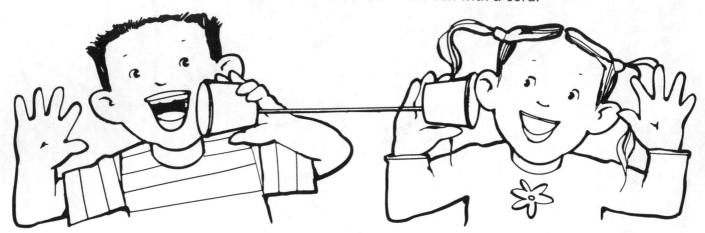

2. Invite students to make their own old-fashioned telephones.
   a. Give each student a paper cup. Show students how to use a pencil point to poke a tiny hole in the bottom of their cup.
   b. Divide the class into pairs. Give each pair a long piece of kite string.
   c. Show students how to thread the string through the holes and tie a knot to keep it in place.
   d. Have partners stand apart, pulling the string taut, while one student speaks into the cup and the other holds up the cup to his or her ear and listens. Give students time to play with their phones, and encourage them to see how softly they can speak and still be heard.

3. Gather the class together and tell them that they are going to play a different kind of telephone game. Explain that students must first help you write messages that begin with the words *A good citizen*. Discuss with students what it means to be a good citizen. Let each student have a turn finishing one message. Write the messages on slips of paper, and put the paper slips in a hat.

4. Invite the class to sit in a circle. Then explain the rules of the game.
   a. You will choose one student to be the "operator."
   b. The operator draws a message from the hat, reads it silently, and then whispers it to the student sitting on his or her right. The message cannot be repeated.
   c. The student who heard the message then whispers it to the next student. This continues until the message moves completely around the circle and back to the operator.
   d. The operator then stands and repeats what he or she heard. Chances are it will be very different from the original message!
   e. Finally, the operator reads the message on the slip of paper and then chooses the next operator. Play continues until everyone has a turn being the operator.

5. Model how to play the game by being the first operator. Make sure everyone understands the rules. Then start a new round of the game, and help any students who may not be able to read the messages on their own.

6. When the game is over, invite students to share what they think is the most important rule of good citizenship.

Extended Learning

• Discuss with students why it is important to be a good citizen. Invite them to design a Good Citizen Award. Have students give their award to someone at school, at home, or in their neighborhood.

• Invite students to make posters that illustrate the principles of good citizenship. Use the posters for a bulletin board display.

978-1-4129-5932-2

Granny Games

Objective

Students will compare and contrast games played today with games played long ago.

Give students a blast from the past with four games their grandparents might have played when they were children. Show students that some of the best games don't require batteries, electricity, or computers.

Materials

- Granny Games Cards reproducibles
- chart paper
- 2 oranges
- 2 spoons
- clean gallon milk carton
- 20 clothespins
- small plastic ball
- handkerchief

1. Ask students to describe their favorite games. Record their responses on the board, and circle any that use electronics. Ask students: *What games did children play before electronic games were available?* Record their responses, and invite students to compare and contrast the games on the two lists.

2. Tell students they are going to play some games that their grandparents or great-grandparents may have played when they were children. Make a copy of the **Granny Games Cards reproducibles (pages 74–75)**. Create a station for each game. Include the materials needed to play the game and a game card.

3. Introduce one game at a time. Model and explain the rules as follows:

   Orange Wars: Two players compete at a time. Each player holds one spoon with an orange on it. The goal is to knock the opponent's orange off the spoon. Opponents can only touch each other using the one hand that is holding the spoon. The winner is the player who is still holding an orange on the spoon at the end of the game.

978-1-4129-5932-2

Clothespin Drop: Place an empty gallon milk carton on the floor. Each player takes ten clothespins. Players take turns standing next to the carton and dropping clothespins into it. They must hold the clothespins at waist level. The winner is the player who drops the most pins into the carton.

Wind Storm: Players are grouped into two teams. Teams kneel at opposite ends of a large table. They place a small plastic ball in the middle of the table. Both teams blow the ball as hard as they can, trying to blow it off the opposing team's side of the table. Teams earn one point each time they succeed in blowing the ball past the opposing team and off of the table. The first team to score ten points wins the game.

The Cat's Meow: One player is chosen as "It" and ties a handkerchief around his or her eyes as a blindfold. "It" stands in the middle of a rug or designated play area. The other players move around the inside of the play area as "It" tries to tag them. When a player is tagged, he or she must meow like a cat. "It" listens to the sound of the meow and tries to guess which player it is. If the guess is correct, the tagged player becomes the new "It."

4. After modeling each game, divide the class into four groups. Assign each group to a game station. After about 15 minutes, have groups rotate to the next station. Continue until each group has played each game.

5. Close the activity by bringing the class back together again. Have students discuss the games and tell what they liked or didn't like about each one. Ask them to compare and contrast these games to the ones they like to play.

Extended Learning

- Ask students to brainstorm a list of questions about games children played long ago. Encourage them to use the questions to interview a grandparent or an older neighbor. Have students share their interviews with the class.

- Have students work in small groups to create a new game that does not use any electronics. Invite groups to teach their games to the class.

Granny Games Cards

Orange Wars

Number of Players: 2
What You Need:

How to Play:

1. Choose someone to play with.
2. Hold a spoon in one hand.
3. Put an orange on your spoon.
4. Try to knock the orange off the other player's spoon. You can only use the hand holding the spoon.

Pin Drop

Number of Players: 1 or more
What You Need:

 10

How to Play:

1. Stand next to the milk carton.
2. Hold a clothespin at your waist.
3. Try to drop it in the carton.
4. Do this nine more times.
5. Count how many clothespins you got into the carton.

Granny Games Cards

Wind Storm

Number of Players: 4 or more

What You Need:

How to Play:

1. Choose teams.
2. Each team kneels at one end of the table.
3. Put the ball in the middle of the table.
4. Try to blow the ball off the table on the other team's side. Score one point each time.
5. The first team to get ten points wins.

The Cat's Meow

Number of Players: 4 or more

What You Need:

How to Play:

1. Choose one player to be "It."
2. "It" covers his or her eyes with the handkerchief.
3. "It" tries to tag the other players.
4. When you are tagged, meow like a cat.
5. "It" listens to the meow and tries to guess who it is.
6. If "It" guesses your name, you become the new "It."

"Goods and Services" Match-Up

Materials
- Goods and Services Game Cards reproducibles
- cardstock
- scissors
- resealable plastic bags
- chart paper

Objectives
Students will understand the difference between goods and services. Students will learn that money is used to purchase goods and services.

Does the hairstylist need a toothbrush or a hairbrush? Does the gardener need a lawn mower or a vacuum cleaner? In this game, students match each worker with the appropriate object as they test their knowledge of goods and services.

1. Ahead of time, copy the **Goods and Services Game Cards reproducibles (pages 78–79)** on cardstock. Make one copy of each page for every two students. Cut out the cards, and place each set of cards in a resealable plastic bag.

2. Ask students to name items that they or their families buy that can be touched or held. Tell students that these are examples of *goods*. List their suggestions on chart paper.

3. Then ask students to name services that they or their families use. Explain that a *service* is work that someone does for you. Giving someone a haircut, broadcasting a weather report on TV, or delivering mail to homes and business are all examples of services people provide. List students' suggestions on another sheet of chart paper.

4. Tell students that they will play "Goods and Services" Match-Up. Divide the class into pairs. Give each pair one bag of game cards.

5. Model and explain the rules of the game.
   a. The object of the game is to match picture cards of goods with the people who provide the related services (e.g., toothbrush and dentist).
   b. One player shuffles the cards and deals four cards facedown to each player. The dealer places the rest of the cards facedown in a stack. This is the draw pile.
   c. The dealer turns over the top card of the draw pile and places it next to the pile. This is the discard pile.

d. Players look at their cards but do not show them to anyone else. If players have a matching good and service card, they place the pair faceup on the table.

e. Players take turns drawing a card from the draw pile or the discard pile. If the card matches one of the cards in the player's hand, he or she places the matching cards faceup on the table. Then the player's turn is over and he or she discards one card.

f. At the beginning of each turn, players should have four cards in their hands. If not, players draw the number of cards needed to have four cards. Then they draw one more card to start their turn.

g. When no more cards are in the draw pile, one player shuffles the cards in the discard pile and places them facedown to start a new draw pile. He or she then turns over the top card to start a new discard pile.

h. The game is over when all matches have been made. The player with the most matches wins.

6. Model playing several hands with a volunteer. Show students your cards, and ask them to identify any matches. Then have pairs play independently. Circulate around the room to answer any questions or provide assistance.

7. As a follow-up, ask students to choose a service card and name goods that are associated with it. Challenge them to name at least five goods for each service.

Extended Learning

- Encourage students to set up a classroom store. Make a list of services the students can perform for the class. Then let them visit the store to use their classmates' services. Provide props for students to use as goods.

- Have students collect ads from stores and markets. Then ask them to make collages of goods they would like to buy.

Goods and Services Game Cards

Goods and Services Game Cards

CHAPTER 5

Physical Education, Art, and Music

Animal Antics

Objectives
Students will practice using different locomotor movements.
Students will mimic the movements of animals.

Students love playing Follow the Leader, especially when they get to be the leader! In this variation of the classic, visual prompts encourage students to incorporate different types of locomotor movements into the game.

1. Get students excited about this game by inviting them to mimic different animal movements. Call out a movement, such as *hopping* or *slithering*. Ask students to name animals that use these movements and demonstrate how the movements might look. Then name animals and challenge students to name and demonstrate several movements for each one.

2. Next, make a copy of the **Animal Antics reproducibles (pages 82–83)**. Cut out the cards, and display them one at a time to the class. Have students identify each animal, and challenge them to describe three or four movements the animal might make.

3. Then tell students they are going to play a game similar to Follow the Leader. Divide the class into two teams. Give each team one copy of the Animal Antics reproducibles. Have teams cut out the cards and color the pictures. Then ask them to tape each picture to a separate plastic cone.

Materials
- Animal Antics reproducibles
- scissors
- crayons or markers
- 24 plastic cones or other markers
- tape
- whistle

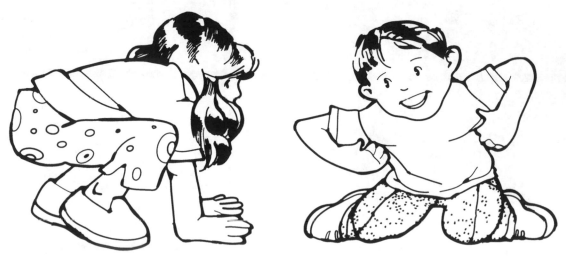

4. Have the teams spread out their plastic cones over a large, designated play area. Then have each team line up behind a starting line. Model and explain the game rules:

  a. The first person in line is the leader. (Students can vote on a leader or you can appoint one.) The leader looks at the picture on the first cone, identifies the animal, and chooses a movement to imitate the animal.

  b. Then the leader leads his or her team around the play area using that movement. Each time the leader gets to a new cone, he or she must immediately change movements to match the new animal.

  c. The rest of the team must follow the leader in a line, mimicking the leader's movements.

  d. At some point during the game, blow a whistle. Teams must pick up all their cones and place each cone in a new spot.

  e. When you blow the whistle again, teams run to the starting line and line up again. The previous leader goes to the end of the line. The new leader stands at the beginning of the line.

5. Play one practice round to be sure everyone understands the rules. When you blow the whistle, watch to ensure that students move each cone to a new area and that teams line up again with a new leader. Make sure each team member gets the opportunity to lead.

6. After the game, ask students to identify other animal movements they can add to the game.

Extended Learning

• Set up an obstacle course that requires students to crawl over and under objects and move forward, backward, and sideways.

• Play a music CD that features a variety of tempos and rhythms. As students move around the play area, have them change the speed of their movements to match the tempo of the music.

Animal Antics

Animal Antics

Catch It if You Can!

Objective

Students will throw and catch balls from different distances.

Materials
- playground balls
- chalk

A game of catch seems simple enough, but students will have to use their brains if they want to stay in this game. As partners move farther apart, they must make important decisions. Should they throw underhand or overhand? How hard should they throw the ball? Give three cheers for the last team standing—and catching!

1. Get students warmed up for this game by giving each student a ball. At your signal, have students repeatedly toss their ball up in the air and catch it. As students drop their balls, have them sit off to the side until there is only one player left.

2. Next, take students outside to a play area. Divide the class into pairs. Give each pair a playground ball and a piece of chalk.

3. Have one student from each pair stand along a line on the playground. Students should be at least two arms' length apart from each other. Then have the other students face their partners and take one giant step backward.

4. Model and explain the rules of the game.
   a. The object of the game is for partners to throw and catch a ball from as far a distance as possible.

978-1-4129-5932-2

b. Students who are standing on the line toss the ball underhand to their partner. If the partner catches the ball, he or she takes one giant step backward and tosses the ball back to the line. This continues until a student cannot catch the ball.

c. When catching the ball, the student is only allowed to move one foot. The other foot must stay in place or the catch does not count.

d. When a student is unable to catch a ball, partners mark the ground with chalk to show how far apart they were. The student standing on the line draws a line behind his or her partner's heels.

e. The game is over when the last pair of students can no longer catch the ball.

5. Make sure everyone understands the rules. As students begin playing, remind them that the person catching the ball must keep one foot in place.

6. After the game, have one student stand on the line while his or her partner stands on the chalk mark. Encourage students to compare and contrast the differences in distance for each pair.

Extended Learning

- Use plastic cones to set up an obstacle course. Have students practice ball-control skills, such as kicking and dribbling, as they move through the course.

- Invite volunteers to demonstrate how balls are used in different sports, such as baseball, basketball, football, tennis, volleyball, and golf.

Take a Look! Guessing Game

Materials

- *Look Book* by Tana Hoban
- nature magazines and books
- paintbrushes
- tempera paint
- 8" white and black paper squares
- die-cut shapes (e.g., circles, squares, triangles)
- scissors
- stapler

Objectives

Students will describe and replicate patterns found in nature.
Students will create original artwork for use in a class book.

After exploring the photographs in Tana Hoban's *Look Book*, students will search for subjects found in nature. They will paint their subjects and compile the paintings into a class book styled after Hoban's work.

1. Get students interested in this game by showing them *Look Book* by Tana Hoban. Each photograph in the book is first presented with only a small portion shown through a die-cut shape. Encourage students to study what they see and then predict what the total photograph will show. There are several other books by Hoban that follow this same format, including *Just Look* and *Take Another Look*.

2. Tell students that they will work together to create a type of art game, much like Hoban's books. Let students look through nature magazines and books to find a photograph of a subject. Encourage them to look for subjects that have some kind of pattern, such as a zebra's stripes or a flower's petals.

3. Give students an eight-inch white paper square, and invite them to paint their subject on the paper.

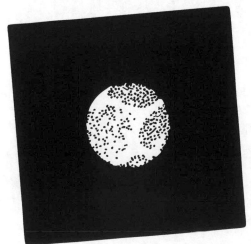 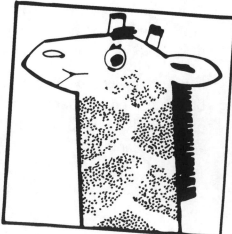

4. After the paintings have dried, give students an eight-inch black paper square. Have students study their painting and decide which portion they will show through a cutout in their black square. Then have them trace a die-cut shape onto the black square in the appropriate place and cut it out. Help students staple the black paper over their painting along one side.

5. Invite each student to present his or her painting to the class. Encourage the class to discuss the patterns they see in the cutout and predict what the whole painting will show. When a student guesses correctly, the full painting is revealed. The student who guesses the subject of the painting gets to be the next presenter.

6. After the presentations, collect students' paintings. Group the paintings into stacks of five or six, and have the class help you bind them into books. Invite students from other classes to borrow the class books and see how many subjects they can identify.

Extended Learning

- Have students collect leaves and make leaf rubbings. Then place the collected leaves in a box, and challenge students to match them with the rubbings.

- Use objects found in nature as props in a lesson on the elements of art. For example, use plants and flowers to discuss lines and shapes, and use sand and sheep's wool to discuss texture. Encourage students to discuss how they would depict the objects in a painting or drawing.

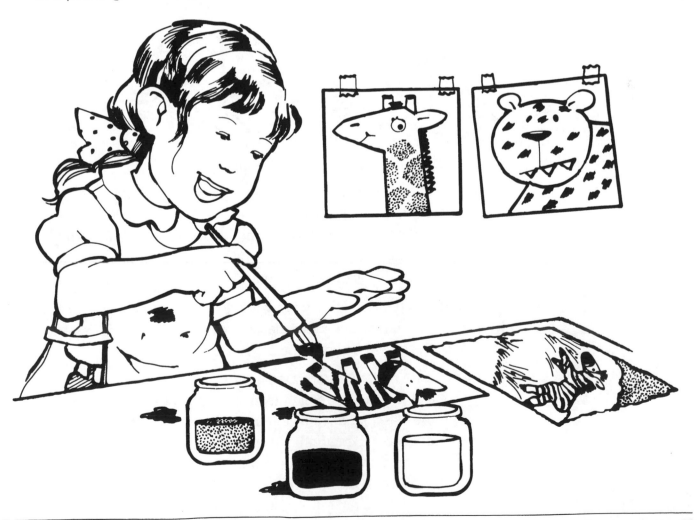

Picture This! Everyday Art

Materials
- crayons
- drawing paper
- old magazines or calendars

Objective
Students will work together to create artwork based on everyday experiences and individual perspectives.

Let students express their artistic side with this engaging, artistic game. Everyone will draw an object based on the same description. What will each artist picture in his or her mind? Students will be amazed to see how one description can produce such different results.

1. Invite students to stand in front of a classroom window. Give a one-sentence description of something you see outside. Be as specific as possible. For example, you might say: *I see a brown tree with rough bark and soft green leaves.* Ask students how they could show that description in a drawing.

2. Invite volunteers to describe other elements of the scene. They might say things such as: *There is an old, red backpack under the tree,* or *The gray sky is filled with thin, dark clouds.* After each description, have students share what techniques they might use to show those elements in a drawing. For example, they might use thin, black lines to show clouds.

3. Tell students that they are going to play a cooperative art game. Have them arrange their desks and chairs in straight rows. Give each student crayons and a sheet of drawing paper.

4. Choose a picture from a magazine or calendar. Select a picture of a scene with several objects in it. Do not show the picture to the class. Model how to play the game by acting as the first "storyteller." Explain the following rules to the class:

   a. The storyteller chooses a picture and describes one element, or piece, of the picture.

b. The students are the artists. They draw the described element on their papers.

c. When everyone has finished drawing the first element, the storyteller says: *Pass.* Artists pass their paper to the student seated behind them. The last person in each row will bring his or her paper to the first person in the row.

d. Then the storyteller describes another element of the scene, and the artists draw it on the paper that was passed to them.

e. This process continues until the artists have their original papers again. Students will be fascinated to see how each student interpreted and drew each element.

f. Choose a new storyteller and picture for the next game, and play again.

5. At the end of the game, collect the drawings and display them at students' eye level. Encourage students to compare and contrast the drawings. Then display the original pictures, and have students compare them to their own artwork.

Extended Learning

- Set up a still-life display in your classroom. Have students sit in a circle around it and paint what they see from where they are seated, each from a different perspective.

- Have each student choose a photograph of a landscape. Encourage students to develop artwork based on their photograph using different techniques, such as painting, sculpture, and collage.

Name That Instrument

Materials

- Name That Instrument reproducibles
- computer with Internet access
- scissors
- crayons
- tape
- craft sticks
- samples of different instruments on CD (optional)
- CD player (optional)

Objective

Students will identify symphony instruments by sound.

In this game, students will become "music detectives" as they try to identify musical instruments based only on the sounds they make. Who will have an ear for music and take "note" of the clues? Play the game and find out!

1. Get students excited about the game by having them explore Internet Web sites featuring musical instruments. As always, thoroughly investigate any Web site providing access for students. Choose a site that shows pictures of instruments and offers short samples of what the instruments sound like. A good Web site to use is from the Dallas Symphony Orchestra at: *www.dsokids. com/2001/instrumentchart.htm.*

2. After students have had time to hear the sounds of different instruments, invite them to discuss what they have learned. Have them share the names of the instruments they listened to and describe how the sounds are made. Help students categorize instruments into these families: strings, percussion, woodwinds, brass, and keyboards. Create a chart on the board.

3. Divide the class into teams of five. Give each team a set of picture cards from the **Name That Instrument reproducibles (pages 92–93)**. Have teams color and tape the cards to craft sticks.

4. Ask teams to assign each player to a different family of instruments. That student becomes the team expert on that family. Then model and explain the rules of the game.
   a. Each team sits together during the game.
   b. Experts collect the picture cards for their family of instruments and place them on the table.
   c. Use the computer or a CD player to play a sample of music from one instrument.

978-1-4129-5932-2

d. The first team to hold up the picture card that identifies the correct instrument scores one point.

e. Record points on the board.

f. The first team to score ten points wins the game.

5. Play a few practice rounds to make sure students understand how to play the game. Then begin a real game. Make sure students hear the same instrument several times to reinforce learning and listening skills.

6. At the end of the game, have students name their favorite instrument and tell what they like about it. Invite them to share experiences they have had with music, such as attending concerts or listening to CDs at home.

Extended Learning

- Play a recording of Sergei Prokofiev's *Peter and the Wolf*. Challenge students to identify the musical instruments they hear.

- Have students sort pictures of musical instruments by families, such as strings, percussion, and woodwinds.

Name That Instrument

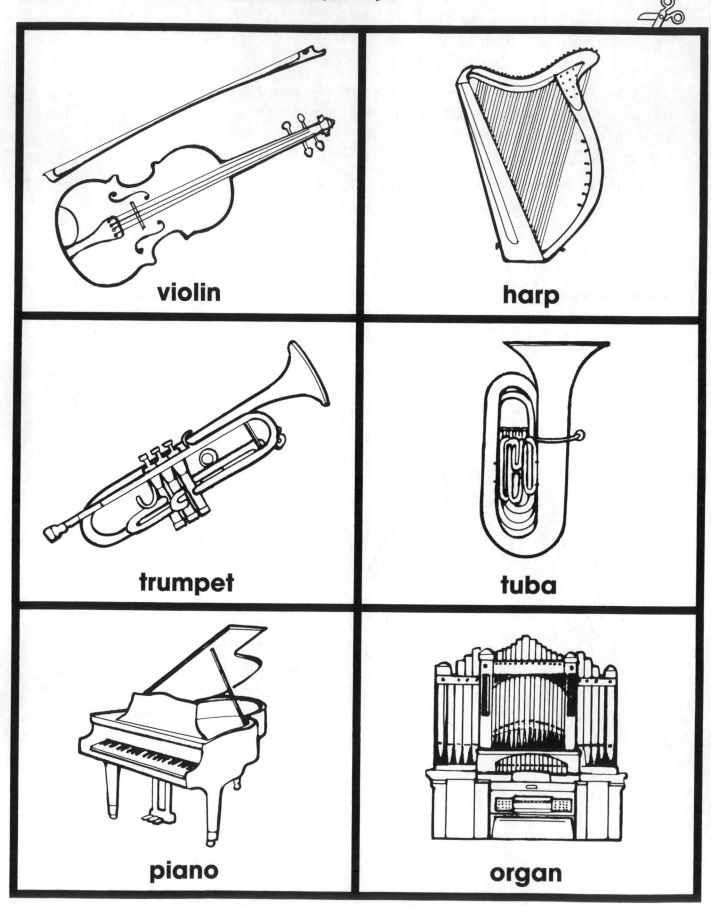

violin

harp

trumpet

tuba

piano

organ

Reproducible 978-1-4129-5932-2 • © *Corwin Press*

Name That Instrument

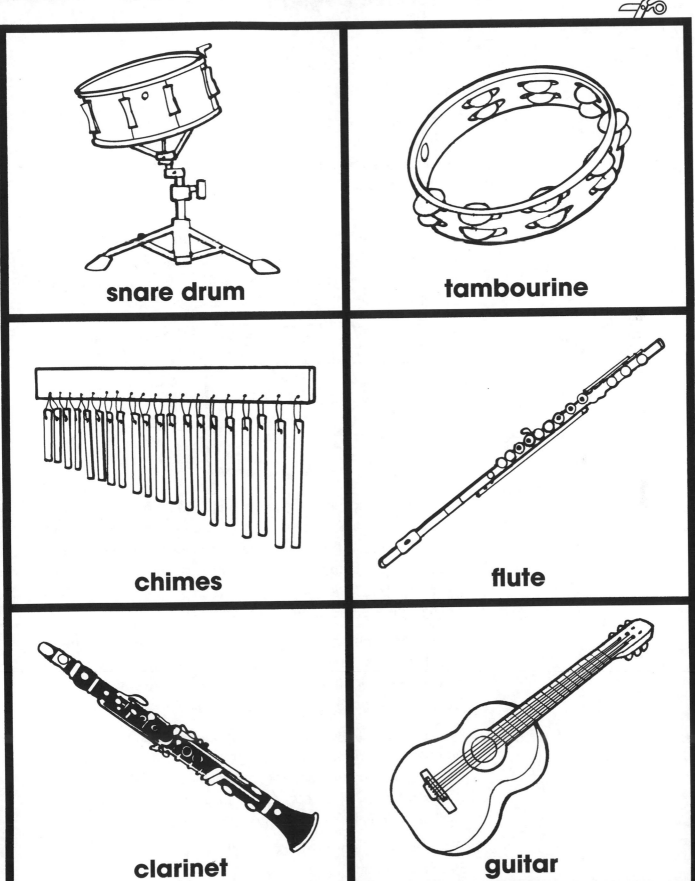

snare drum

tambourine

chimes

flute

clarinet

guitar

The Twelve Days of School

Materials

- recording of the song "The Twelve Days of Christmas"
- CD or cassette player
- chart paper
- ball

Objectives

Students will create new lyrics for a classic song.
Students will remember the order of the words in a counting song.

In this game, students will enjoy creating and then trying to remember new lyrics for a favorite holiday song. Instead of turtle doves and lords a-leaping, students will sing about familiar school tools such as books and erasers. They will then play a game to see if they can remember all the words to their new song.

1. As students are coming into the classroom after recess, play a recording of "The Twelve Days of Christmas." This activity will be particularly intriguing if you do this in a month that is nowhere near December.

2. Have students listen to the song, and then help you list the twelve gifts on a sheet of chart paper (*a partridge in a pear tree, two turtle doves, three French hens, four calling birds, five gold rings, six geese a-laying, seven swans a-swimming, eight maids a-milking, nine ladies dancing, ten lords a-leaping, eleven pipers piping,* and *twelve drummers drumming*).

3. Next, tell students they are going to rewrite the lyrics of the song to tell about the first twelve days of school. Model how to do this by teaching them this new verse: *On the first day of school, my teacher gave to me, a nametag on my new desk.*

4. Divide the class into eleven small groups. Assign each group one number, from two to twelve. Ask groups to write a new verse to the song for the number they are assigned. Circulate among the groups, and ask which school tool they chose. List the items on the board to make sure each group uses a different item.

5. When all the groups are done, line them up in numerical order. Have each group sing its verse. List the gifts on a new sheet of chart paper.

6. Practice singing the song as a group. Sing it through a few times to make sure everyone knows all of the words.

7. Now, tell students they are going to play a circle game using their song. Invite students to sit on the floor. Hold a ball, and explain the rules of the game.

   a. The student holding the ball starts the game. He or she begins singing the song from the verse that begins: *On the twelfth day of school, my teacher gave to me, twelve . . .*

   b. Once all twelve gifts have been named, the student rolls the ball to someone else. That student then adds the next part of the song, starting with the number *eleven*.

   c. He or she rolls the ball to the next student, and so on, until the group finishes the song.

   d. If a student cannot remember the words for his or her part of the song, he or she must start the song over again from: *On the twelfth day of school . . .*

   e. The game is over when the group successfully sings the whole song, from the twelfth day to the first day.

8. After the game, have groups draw a picture that represents their verse. Hang the pictures on the wall, side-by-side, to create a mural about the first twelve days of school.

Extended Learning

- Have students work in groups to write new lyrics for other familiar songs. Invite groups to perform their songs for the class.

- Gather a collection of song recordings from different cultures. Play a different song each day, and discuss with students the song's mood, tempo, rhythm, and message. Encourage students to draw pictures or write stories to go with the songs.

On the second day of school, my teacher gave to me, two pink erasers!

References

Beyers, J. (1998). The biology of human play. *Child Development, 69*(3), 599–600.

Bjorkland, D. F., & Brown, R. D. (1998). Physical play and cognitive development: Integrating activity, cognition, and education. *Child Development, 69*(3), 604–606.

Burpee®. (2007). *Seed catalog.* Retrieved April 12, 2007, from http://www.burpee.com.

California Department of Education. (2005). *History-social science framework for California public schools, kindergarten through grade 12.* Sacramento, CA: California Department of Education.

California Department of Education. (2006). *Mathematics framework for California public schools, kindergarten through grade 12.* Sacramento, CA: California Department of Education.

California Department of Education. (1994). *Physical education framework for California public schools, kindergarten through grade 12.* Sacramento, CA: California Department of Education.

California Department of Education. (1999). *Reading/language arts framework for California public schools, kindergarten through grade 12.* Sacramento, CA: California Department of Education.

California Department of Education. (2004). *Science framework for California public schools, kindergarten through grade 12.* Sacramento, CA: California Department of Education.

California Department of Education. (2004). *Visual and performing arts framework for California public schools, kindergarten through grade 12.* Sacramento, CA: California Department of Education.

Crawford, R. (1996–2006). *Puzzles.* Retrieved April 17, 2007, from the Tangrams Web site: http://www.tangrams.ca.

Dallas Symphony Association. (2006). *Families of the orchestra.* Retrieved May 6, 2007, from http://www.dsokids.com/2001/instrumentchart.htm.

Gardner, H. (1983). *Frames of mind: The theory of multiple intelligences.* New York, NY: Basic Books.

Jensen, E. (1995). *Brain-based learning and teaching.* Del Mar, CA: The Brain Store.

Jensen, E. (2001). *Arts with the brain in mind.* Alexandria, VA: Association for Supervision and Curriculum Development.

McCarthy, B. (1990). Using the 4MAT system to bring learning styles to schools. *Educational Leadership, 48*(2), 31–37.

National Council for the Social Studies. (2002). *Expectations of excellence: Curriculum standards for social studies.* Silver Spring, MD: National Council for the Social Studies (NCSS).

National Council of Teachers of English and the International Reading Association. (1996). *Standards for the English language arts.* Urbana, IL: National Council of Teachers of English (NCTE).

National Council of Teachers of Mathematics. (2005). *Principles and standards for school mathematics.* Reston, VA: National Council of Teachers of Mathematics (NCTM).

National Research Council. (1996). *National science education standards.* Washington, DC: National Academy Press.

Park® Seed Company. (1997–2007). *Seed catalog.* Retrieved April 12, 2007, from http://www.parkseed.com.

Tate, M. L. (2003). *Worksheets don't grow dendrites: 20 instructional strategies that engage the brain.* Thousand Oaks, CA: Corwin Press.

Wolfe, P. (2001). *Brain matters: Translating research into classroom practice.* Alexandria, VA: Association for Supervision and Curriculum Development.

Printed in the United States
By Bookmasters